From Adam to Isa:
Stories of the Brothers
of the Prophet Muhammad

(peace be upon them all)

Dr Abdul Qader Ismail

Written by Dr Abdul Qader Ismail BMBCh (Oxon), MA (Oxon), MRCPCH, under the spiritual guidance of Khawaja Muhammad Ulfat Qadri Naqshbandi (Lahore, Pakistan), and Pir Mohammad Tayyab Ur-Rahman Qadri (Qadria Trust, UK; Bhera Shareef, Haripur, Pakistan).

The main source of information for this book was *'Stories Of The Prophets (Peace Be Upon Them)'* by *Imam Imaduddin Abul-Fida Isma'il Ibn Kathir Ad-Dimashqi* (ISBN 9960-892-26-3).

Jazak'Allah Khair to everyone who helped proofread the text and made helpful suggestions.

Front cover photo: Aerial shot of Masjid'al-Aqsa

Masjid'al-Aqsa is not the name of a single Mosque, but an area / compound that contains five Mosques (Qibli Mosque, Buraq Mosque, Dome of the Rock Mosque, Marwani Mosque, and Old Aqsa basement Mosque). On the night of the Isra w'al-Mi'raj, the Prophet Muhammad led all of the Prophets of Allah, from Adam to Isa (peace be upon them all) in prayer, as their Imam, in Masjid'al-Aqsa. The Prophet Muhammad (peace be upon him) said, "… There is not a single inch in al-Quds (Jerusalem) where a Prophet has not prayed or an Angel not stood." (Tirmidhi)

Designed by: Toqeer Bhatti
www.synergidigital.com

For all our Muslim brothers and sisters going through trials and tribulations. May Allah grant them patience and relief.

Table of Contents

Foreword

Dr Abdul Qader Ismail is a gifted Muslim doctor, a graduate of the University of Oxford, a writer and a pious, caring person. His new book '**From Adam to Isa: Stories of the Brothers of the Prophet Muhammad**' is a welcome addition to the library of any pious Muslim household. Dr Ismail is keen to ensure that our children receive good Islamic education, and he has now selected the stories of the Prophets who are mentioned in the Qur'an.

Stories in the Quran

Why does the Qur'an tell so many stories? Ibn Kathir, in his famous book 'Al-Bidaya wa'l-Nihaya,' tells in detail more than 150 stories of the 25 Prophets mentioned in Qur'an. These historical stories provide insights into the human condition: disobedience, ungratefulness, jealousy, and miserliness. They contain moral lessons that help us to reflect on our own lives. They shed light on how Allah

has always sought to guide humanity through His chosen Prophets, but how the majority of them were rejected. The stories describe human wretchedness and rebellion against accepting the truth. We see Divine retribution in the form of severe punishment in many cases, but also the rescuing of the faithful. The Prophets and their followers are presented as role models for humanity.

The purpose of Prophetic stories

Allah says, *"We will tell you the most beautiful story by revealing to you this Qur'an, a story of which you were unaware before."* (Qur'an 12:3) The Qur'an appears to recycle and repeat the same two dozen stories. However, a discerning look shows that whenever it repeats a story there is a new bit, a new twist or lesson, a new setting and context.

◆ The Qur'an tells stories to give the readers guidance and teachings about Allah's kindness and forgiveness. After telling the story of Prophet Yusuf in detail, the Qur'an sums up its purpose, *"In the story of Yusuf and his brothers, there is a lesson for those who understand. It isn't a made-up account, but confirmation of what happened in the past, it explains all things, a guidance that is useful for those who believe."* (Qur'an 12:111)

◆ The stories about the Prophets highlight on the one hand human stubbornness and history of disobedience. These stories mention numerous gifts that Allah blessed humanity with but humans continue to be ungrateful for. On the other hand, they illustrate Allah's justice in how He will ensure that oppression and human barbarity will be dealt with. This points to the need for the Day of Judgement and afterlife.

◆ The Quran says *"We tell you the stories of the messengers to make your heart strong, and what has come to you in this account is the truth, teachings and a reminder for the believers."* (Qur'an 11:120) These stories were a source of consolation for the Prophet Muhammad who faced opposition from his people, being mocked and persecuted. He, and his followers are reassured that, like the previous communities they will be the winners in the end.

Dr Ismail's book will be a good introduction to these Qur'anic stories. May Allah bless him and give him *Tawfiq* to continue this service for the next generation of Muslims.

Dr Musharraf Hussain OBE, DL [i]

---

[i]   Translator of the Majestic Quran, www.majesticquran.co.uk

Introduction

The Prophet Muhammad (peace be upon him) said, "...The Prophets are paternal brothers; their mothers are different, but their religion is one." (Bukhari)

It is vital for young Muslims to know the context within which the Qur'an was revealed to the Prophet Muhammad (peace be upon him). This context is provided by teaching them about the lives of previous Prophets and explaining how they were all Muslims bringing a version of Islam as befitted their societies, with revelations all revealed by the same, unchanging, one true God, Allah. Understanding this context, this brotherhood of Prophets, grants a deep realisation of Islam's relationship with other world religions, especially Judaism and Christianity, the other Abrahamic faiths. Near the end of the book is a chapter that explicitly deals with the question of why there are so many religions in the world today.

The lives of the Prophets contain everything children want in a story, perilous adventures and impossible missions, dastardly and dangerous villains, miraculous superpowers and

mighty heroes, Angels and Devils, punishments and rewards, morals and lessons. Most importantly, they are true stories, from ancient human history, that children can claim ownership of as being part of their history and feel proud of knowing and learning from.

Each story contains countless lessons, and so I withstood the temptation to provide a list of questions or learning points. I would rather the child reflect on the story and consider what lessons they can draw from it, relevant to their age, level of understanding, and society in which they live (with help from their parents or teachers). In this way, the stories can be revisited repeatedly as the child grows, physically, intellectually and emotionally.

Every book on the lives of the Prophets is a book of *Salawat*. Repeatedly, after mentioning the name of the Prophets, the reader will make supplication for Allah to send His peace and blessings upon them. However, in a book for children, where the information is presented as a story, this can be disruptive, especially when Prophet's names may appear several times in one sentence. To avoid this, I have followed a system whereby a supplication for sending peace and blessings is included the first time a Prophet's name is mentioned in each paragraph, and not thereafter. Furthermore, to enhance this element and make it more obvious, each chapter ends with a short *Salawat* slightly more specific to its Prophet(s).

Finally, I included some additional chapters not normally found in books on the lives of the Prophets (peace be upon them all), but that I felt were necessary and valuable. This includes chapters on Allah, Angels, Jinn, Paradise and Hell.

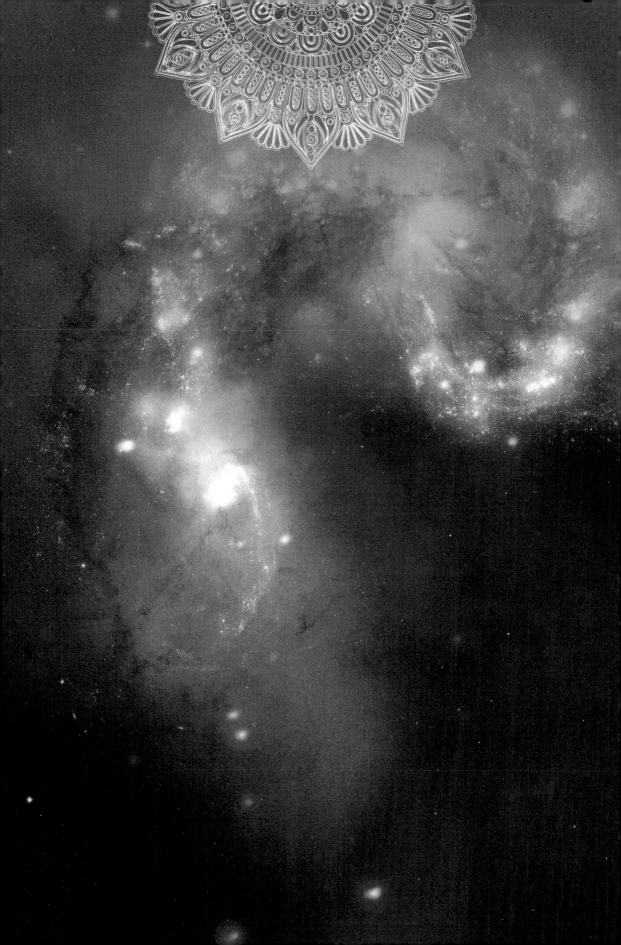

Allah

Allah is the one and only God, the Creator and Sustainer of everything. Allah is the only true Reality, there is no reality except for Him. Everything apart from Him is like a shadow, or a dream – it only exists because of Him and cannot exist without Him. Anything and everything only exists because of His creating and sustaining it every moment of its existence. If He was to stop sustaining it for even a moment, it would instantly vanish out of existence. Allah is infinite, eternal, immortal, invulnerable. Allah is The All knowing (omniscient). Time is one of His creations and He is not affected by it. Therefore, for Him there is no past, present or future. His knowledge is such, that it is impossible for there to be anything outside of His knowledge, even before it came into existence. This includes our most secret thoughts and emotions which even we may not be aware of. Allah says that if all the trees on the earth were turned into pens and the water of the seven oceans was turned into ink, and another seven oceans worth of ink was added to it, we would still not be able to record Allah's knowledge.

Allah is The All Powerful (omnipotent). His power is such, that there is no other power except His, i.e., nothing else has any power. Therefore, nothing can and does happen unless it is His will. Allah says that if the whole world was to come together to try and benefit us in some way, they would not be able to benefit us unless Allah wills it to be so, and if they were to come together to try and harm us in some way, they would not be able to do so unless it was according to Allah's will. And when Allah wills something, all He does is say 'Be!' – and it is.

Furthermore, Allah does not depend on His creation for anything, nor can His creation benefit or harm Him in any way. If everyone who ever lived (human and Jinn) believed in Him, worshipped Him, and were as pious as the Prophets of Allah, this would not increase Him in any way. And if everyone who ever lived (human and Jinn) disbelieved in Him, and were as sinful and ungrateful as the Shaitan, this would not decrease Him in any way.

Allah is the King of kings, Lord of all the worlds. His kingdom contains the entirety of creation. Currently, nearly 8 billion people live on Earth. Scientists estimate that if we were to count every person who was ever born, it would be nearly 120 billion. And who knows how many more people will be born before the Day of Judgement. Allah tells us that if all of humanity, from the time of the Prophet Adam (peace be upon him) to the Day of Judgement was to stand before Him and ask for whatever they wanted, whatever they could imagine, and He was to grant it to them, this would not decrease Allah's Kingdom in any way.

Another way to understand the size of Allah's kingdom is to consider the size of the Universe. Space is so big that its unit of measurement is not a metre or kilometre, but a light-year. This is the distance light travels in one year. Light is the fastest thing in the Universe, and travels at a speed of nearly 300,000 kilometres every second. In one year, light travels 9 trillion kilometres. Using powerful telescopes, scientists can see faraway galaxies. From their calculations, they estimate the size of the Universe is 93 billion light years (but this is only what we can see, not the actual size of the Universe, which is probably many times bigger). Scientists estimate that the Universe contains 2 trillion galaxies, each of which contains roughly 100 billion stars, like our Sun. Allah tells us that the whole Universe is contained within the first Heaven, and there are seven Heavens in total. The size of the first Heaven compared to the second Heaven is like a tiny ring in a massive desert. And the size of the second Heaven compared to the third Heaven is like a tiny ring in a massive desert, and so on and so forth, until we reach the seventh Heaven. This itself is like a tiny ring in a massive desert compared to the *Kursi* (the Footstool), which is like a ring in a desert when compared to the *Arsh* (the Throne). Consider then, the great-

ness of Allah, for whom all of His creation is like one of us looking at a tiny mustard seed in the palm of our hand.

Allah says He was a hidden treasure and wanted to be known, and this is why He created the creation. Allah says He created the Jinn and Humankind to worship Him. And He sent Prophets with Revelation to tell us about Himself, to tell us how to worship Him, how to live together in peace and harmony, and how to reach His Paradise after we die. He did this because, despite His omnipotence and infinite nature, Allah knows each and every one of us, including me and you, better than our best friends and family know us. And He loves and cares about each and every one of us, including me and you, more than our own parents love us and care for us.

O Allah, You are peace and from You is peace. Blessed are You, the Majestic and Noble. [i]

---

i   Sahih Muslim.

Mala'ikah

Allah created Mala'ikah (Angels) to carry out His orders (even though He is the All Powerful and could do everything Himself). The first Angels were created long before humans and more Angels are created all the time. Angels are made of light, they are neither male nor female, do not need to eat or drink, and are immortal.

Very few people have seen what Angels really look like, but they can change their appearance depending on what they are doing. Allah describes how they took on the form of handsome young men when they visited the Prophet Ibrahim and the Prophet Lut (peace be upon them both). The Prophet Muhammad told us that sometimes, when the Archangel Jibra'il (peace be upon them both) would visit him, he would come in the form of one of his

most handsome companions, Dihya al-Kalbi (may Allah be pleased with him).

Their appearance depends on the person they are visiting. For example, when the Angel of Death, Izra'il (peace be upon him) comes to take the life of a non-Muslim he will have 12 eyes, each flashing like lightning, and with a voice like thunder. He will have a huge stature like a giant, and be black in colour. His hair will be long, reaching his feet, and he will have an unbearable stench. His teeth will be long and sharp, and fire will come from his mouth and nostrils. In his hands he will hold a huge forked mace made of the Fire of Hell. When he strikes the dead person with this mace, it will pierce his body and soul and then he will drag his soul from his body like dragging wet wool over a thorny bush. In contrast to this, when Izra'il comes to take the life of a pious Muslim, he will have a beautiful, smiling form.

Angels have wings, some two, some four, up to 600 and maybe even more. The Prophet Muhammad (peace be upon him) told us that when Allah gives an order, the Angels in the Heavens beat their wings and the sound is like that of a chain hitting rocks. With these wings Angels can fly and they are faster than we can imagine. When the Prophet Ibrahim had laid his son, the Prophet Ismail down and was about to sacrifice him, Allah commanded Jibra'il (peace be upon them all) to replace him with a ram from Paradise. So Jibra'il had to fly from his station at *Sidrat'al-Muntaha* to Paradise, and then fly through the

seven Heavens to where the sacrifice was taking place, all before the knife cut into the Prophet Ismail's neck.

Angels are different sizes and can also change their size depending on the appearance they take on. When Jibra'il came to the Prophet Muhammad (peace be upon them both) in his true form he had 600 wings and filled the entire sky. The Angels who carry the Arsh (the Throne) are so huge that from their earlobe to their shoulder is the distance of 700 years.

There are so many Angels we cannot even begin to imagine their numbers. Every person, from the time of the Prophet Adam (peace be upon him) until the Day of Judgement has two Angels who write down everything they do. There are also Angels whose job it is to protect every person from that which Allah has not written in their destiny, so they will only die when it is their time and not before. The Ka'bah of the Angels is visited by 70,000 Angels every morning and every evening, and no Angel will get a chance to visit it twice until the Day of Judgement because their turn won't come again. The seven Heavens, each of which is unimaginably huge, are also completely full of Angels.

Angels do not get bored or tired doing that which Allah has created them for, and they do not have the free will Allah has given to humans and Jinn, so they are not able to disobey Allah. The Prophet Muhammad (peace be upon him) told us that Allah has Angels who cry and tremble out of His fear. There are so many of them, the tears

that fall from their eyes fall on other Angels worshipping Allah. There are Angels in prostration, others bowing and others standing in rows since Allah created the Heavens and the Earth, and they have not moved and will not move until the Day of Judgement. On that day Allah will appear in front of them, they will look at Him and even though they have spent every moment since they were created, an eternity in His worship they will say: *"Glory be to You! We have not worshiped You as You deserve to be worshiped!"* Angels also spend their time sending peace and blessings upon the Prophet Muhammad (peace be upon him).

We have been told about the names and jobs of some of the Angels. The four most famous and important Angels are Jibra'il, Mika'il, Israfil and Izra'il (peace be upon them all). Jibra'il is the leader of the Angels, he has been given the most important job of bringing Revelation from Allah to His Prophets. He also helps the Prophets during their lifetime by Allah's command, such as when the Prophet Yusuf (peace be upon him) was thrown into the well he stopped him from getting hurt. When the Prophet Ismail was about to be sacrificed by his father (peace be upon them both), Jibra'il swapped him with a ram from Paradise. He was there when the Prophet Musa (peace be upon him) split the Red Sea in half, when the Israelites were being chased by the Pharaoh and his army. During the life of the Prophet Muhammad, Jibra'il (peace be upon them both) opened his chest and washed his heart with Zamzam, he took the Prophet on the miraculous night journey (the

Isra w'al Mi'raj), and he led an army of Angels to help the Muslims during the battle of Badr.

Mika'il (peace be upon him) is in charge of the weather, the sun, the clouds and rain, wind and snow, and whatever grows on the Earth. So, in the way Jibra'il is in charge of bringing that which gives life to our souls, Mika'il is in charge of bringing that which gives life to our bodies (peace be upon them both). Both of these Angels were also spiritual advisers for the Prophet Muhammad (peace be upon him).

Israfil (peace be upon him) has been given one very important job by Allah. He is the one who will blow *al-Sur* (the horn, like a trumpet) when it is time for the Day of Judgement. The Prophet Muhammad (peace be upon him) told us that since Israfil was given this job he is staring at the *Arsh*, listening carefully, and he has drawn in his breath and has his lips on the horn ready to blow, as if he is worried the command will come before he blinks, his eyes like two shining stars. When he blows the trumpet every living thing will die, including the Angel of Death, and then Allah will ask three times, *'Who is King today?'* answering Himself – *'It is Allah – the One, the Irresistible!'* Israfil will be resurrected and will blow the trumpet a second time, bringing everything back to life for the Day of Judgement.

Izra'il (peace be upon him) is the Angel of Death. He, and his helpers are responsible for taking the life of every person when they die. Other Angels include those that carry the *Arsh* of Allah. Malik is the leader of the Angels

in charge of Hell (and is said to never smile) and Ridwan is the leader of the Angels in charge of Paradise. Munkar and Nakir are the two Angels that will ask everyone who dies the three questions of the grave. The *Kiraman Katibin* ('respected scribes') are two Angels who sit on the shoulders of every person writing down everything we do from the time we are born until we die.

There are Angels who pray for the believers who do good deeds. Angels also pray for forgiveness for those people who repent to Allah, and there are Angels that search for places where people have come together to remember Allah and surround them with their wings all the way up to the first Heaven.

What all of this tells us is that the creation of Allah is so vast we cannot even begin to imagine it. What we can see and what we know about is but a tiny fraction. The entire world of Angels is hidden from us but even though we cannot see them, Angels are all around us, especially those people who spend their time doing good deeds and remembering Allah.

O Allah, shower peace and blessings upon Syedina Jibra'il, Mika'il, Israfil, and Izra'il, as much as the number of Your Angels, the level of their obedience, and the extent of their worship.

Jinn

Jinn are another creation of Allah that are similar in some ways to humans, but different in others. Whereas humans were created from clay, Jinn were created from smokeless fire. Jinn were created long before humans and have lived on the Earth for much longer than us. Shaitan is a Jinn called Iblis. Some scholars say he is the father of the Jinn in the way the Prophet Adam (peace be upon him) is the father of humanity. He spent ages worshipping Allah and used to live with the Angels in the Heavens. But when Allah created the Prophet Adam and commanded all the Angels and Iblis to bow down to him, Iblis refused. When Allah asked him why he had disobeyed, he said it was because he was better than Adam, because he was made of fire and Adam was made from clay. Due to his arrogance, Allah punished him by disgracing him and casting him out of Paradise. Instead of realising his mistake and seeking forgiveness from Allah, he blamed Allah for his disobedience, saying it was Allah who led him astray. He asked Allah to give him life until the Day of Judgement (which Allah granted to him) because he was going to make it his mission to lead humanity astray.

Jinn can think and choose what to do, similar to humans and unlike Angels and animals. This means they are also accountable for their actions and will be judged on the Day of Judgement. Like us, Allah says they were created to worship Him. The Prophets of Allah (peace be upon them all) were sent to guide humans and Jinn, and Allah tells us in the Qur'an how some Jinn listened to the Qur'an from the Prophet Muhammad and became Muslims. So like humans, some Jinn choose to be good, worship Allah and follow the Prophets (peace be upon them all) and live peacefully in their societies. But also, like humans, some Jinn choose to be evil, disobey Allah and His Prophets, kill and wage war with each other, and cause mischief and harm to humans. The leader of these Jinn is the Shaitan, and they are called the *Shayatin*.

Shaitan and his followers try and lead people astray by whispering to them to commit evil deeds, waste time, and disobey Allah and His Prophets (peace be upon them all). We cannot see them, we cannot hear them, most of the time we forget they are even there. When they whisper to us, we think it is our own thoughts and feelings. The only way we know these are the whisperings of Shaitan

and his followers is because they will always encourage us to commit sins and refrain from good deeds. They do not get tired and they do not rest. From when we are born, until we die, they will constantly try to make us disobey Allah. What the Shaitan wants most of all is to make us leave the religion of Islam and die as a disbeliever, so we would be sent to Hell for all eternity, just as he will. So Shaitan and his followers are the greatest enemy we have, who are trying to destroy the most precious thing we have, our faith, our Islam. But they cannot force us to do any-thing, they can only lead astray those people who choose to follow them. Furthermore, every person has a *Qareen* (a companion) from among the Angels and from among the Jinn, who encourage them to do good and bad deeds.

The last two Surahs of the Qur'an, *Surah Falaq* and *Surah Nas* are also known as *al-Mu'awidhatayn*. Both of these *Surahs* are a *Dua* in which we ask Allah for protection, so they are a form of *Isti'adha* (to ask Allah for protection from things we cannot see). Once these two *Surahs* were revealed, this was all the Prophet Muhammad (peace be upon him) would recite to ask Allah for protection. When the Prophet would become unwell he would recite these two *Surah*, blow on his hands and rub them over his body. He would also recite them every night before going to sleep and when he woke up each morning. *Surah Nas*, in particular, is asking for protection from the whispering of Shaitan and his followers among people and the Jinn.

Other ways to do this is to recite *Ayat'al-Kursi* or to read the *Ta'awwudh*:

> *Audhu billahi min ash-shaitanir rajeem*
> *I seek refuge in Allah from the accursed Shaitan*

Sometimes, we ask for Allah's protection from the Shaitan but can still feel him whispering to us, distracting us, encouraging us to waste time and sin. This is because these *Dua* are like a weapon in the hand of a warrior. The weapon can be deadly, but if the warrior is weak, he will not be able to defeat his enemy. Similarly, the effectiveness of seeking protection with Allah from the Shaitan is dependent on the level of faith with which we make the *Dua*. However, in the month of Ramadan, the *Shayatin* are chained up and cannot whisper to us.

Jinn are not immortal, but scholars believe they have longer lifespans than humans. They live in places like ruined and deserted buildings and cities, and in dirty places such as bathrooms and garbage dumps, and in graveyards. Disbelieving Jinn also live in homes where Allah is not worshipped. When it gets dark, the Jinn go out of their homes and so this was a time when the Prophet Muhammad (peace be upon him) told parents to keep their children inside.

We do not know exactly what Jinn look like, but we know they have hearts, eyes, ears and tongues. We also know that they eat, drink, laugh, and have families and chil-

dren. We cannot see the Jinn unless they show themselves to us, but they can see us. However, some animals can see them. Jinn can change their shape and make themselves appear to us in different forms. It is likely that all the stories that humans have come up with of mythical and scary beasts, such as fairies, imps, vampires, werewolves, ghosts, poltergeists, demons, UFO (unidentified flying objects), aliens, etc. are Jinn that are playing tricks on, scaring and even killing people. Jinn can also possess people.

Jinn can travel very fast from one place to another, even faster than fighter jets and rockets. They can fly and can even reach space, but meteors and asteroids prevent them from entering the Heavens. They can swim and dive to the bottom of the oceans. Jinn can have the strength of up to 60 humans. The food of the Jinn includes bones. The disbelieving Jinn also eat meat of animals that have been slaughtered without mentioning the name of Allah and drink alcohol. Jinn have animals they ride, and the food for their animals is dung.

Even though most of us will spend our whole life without ever seeing a Jinn, we share our world with them. We also must be constantly on guard against our greatest enemy, the whisperings of Shaitan and his helpers.

Say: "I seek refuge in the Lord of the people, the King of the people, the God of the people, from the evil of the sneaking whisperer, who whispers into people's hearts and minds, from among the Jinn or the people." [ii]

[ii]   Surah Nas (Qur'an 114)

The Prophet Adam
(peace be upon him)

One day, Allah told the Angels that He was going to create a new type of creation that would live on the Earth. Before this, Allah had already created the Jinn and they lived on the Earth. They used to cause mischief and even war with each other, for which Allah would sometimes send the Angels to punish them. So, the Angels assumed this new creation would do the same and respectfully asked Allah why He needed to do this? If it was for His worship, then the Angels already did this constantly without getting tired or needing rest. However, Allah told them that He knew what they did not know.

So, Allah created the Prophet Adam (peace be upon him) from clay harvested from all over the Earth and fashioned his body with His own Hand.[iii] This is why humanity contains people of different races and colours, and different personalities. Adam's body was nearly 30 metres tall. Allah blew Adam's spirit (his soul) into this body, causing him to come alive. Allah taught Adam the names of all things. This could mean that Allah taught the Prophet Adam the name of everything. It could also mean that He gave Adam the ability, the intelligence to be able to think, learn, read, and write, which allowed human beings to learn from their environment and know things they previously did not know. This was something that Allah had not given the Angels, who only knew those things Allah had directly given them knowledge of. Another interpretation could be that Allah gave humanity knowledge of His names and attributes through which they can see Allah's majesty through His creation and get to know Him. After giving life to the Prophet Adam, Allah brought out from him all the souls who were going to be born until the Day of Judgement and took a covenant (a promise) from all of them. He asked them *"Am I not your Lord?"* to which they all replied that He was.

After bringing Adam (peace be upon him) to life, Allah told all the Angels to bow down to him out of respect.

---

iii   Just because Allah has said this in the Qur'an, we do not say that Allah has hands similar to His creation or think about what such hands may be like, and nor do we say Allah doesn't have hands. Any verse of the Qur'an or Hadith which describes Allah in this way (i.e., with body parts or moving from one place to another) is not for us to interpret any further, but just to accept at face value.

Iblis, a Jinn, used to live with the Angels due to his piety, and so was included in this order. While the Angels all obeyed without question or hesitation, Iblis refused out of arrogance, believing himself better than Adam because he was made of fire, while Adam was made of clay. Allah cursed him to become the Shaitan due to his arrogance.

After a period of time, Allah created Hawa (Eve) from Adam's body and the two of them lived as husband and wife in Paradise (peace be upon them both). Allah told them to do whatever they wanted in Paradise but not to approach a specific tree. Shaitan made it his mission to make them disobey Allah, since he blamed Adam as the reason why he had disobeyed Allah. So, he continually whispered to them, convincing them he was their friend, who wanted what was best for them. He persuaded them that eating from that tree wasn't a bad thing, it was a 'Tree of Eternity' that would allow them to live forever in Paradise, close to Allah. Adam and his wife finally gave in. Following the whisperings of Shaitan they ate from the forbidden tree. Upon doing so they immediately recognised the mistake they had made and prayed for forgiveness from Allah. Allah forgave them, but it was now time for humanity to fulfil its destiny to be caretakers of the Earth, and so they left Paradise. Adam lived for a total of 1000 years.

Habil and Qabil

Adam and Hawa (peace be upon them) had many children. They would have two children at a time, twins — one boy and one girl. When their children grew up, the boy in one twin would marry the girl of another twin. It was not allowed for the boy and girl born at the same time as twins to marry each other. Two of Adam's sons were called Habil and Qabil. When they grew up, Habil was meant to marry Qabil's sister, and Qabil was meant to marry Habil's sister. But Qabil thought his own sister was more beautiful than Habil's sister and so wanted to marry her. Their father, Adam, tried to explain to Qabil that this was not allowed and would displease Allah, but Qabil wouldn't listen.

Adam (peace be upon him) told both of them to make a sacrifice to Allah, and whichever sacrifice Allah

accepted would show who was in the right. Habil was a shepherd and he found his best lamb and prepared it for the sacrifice. Qabil was a farmer, but he used his worst crops to prepare the sacrifice. In ancient times, Allah used to show His acceptance of a sacrifice by sending a firestorm. When Habil and Qabil offered their sacrifices the firestorm came, but after it had passed, they saw that Habil's sacrifice had been accepted, while Qabil's sacrifice had been left behind. Instead of accepting this clear sign that he was wrong, Qabil became even more angry and jealous of Habil. He even blamed his father, Adam, of praying only for Habil and not for him.

Qabil became so jealous and angry towards his brother, that he threatened to kill him. Habil explained to him that it wasn't his fault his sacrifice was not accepted, Allah only accepts actions made with sincere intention. If Qabil had been sincere, he would have made a sacrifice of his best crops and would have been ready to accept whatever the outcome was. Instead, Qabil made the sacrifice but was only willing to accept the answer if it proved him right. This meant he was not sincere. Habil also told Qabil that even if he tried to kill him, Habil would not fight with him or hurt him, because he feared Allah and knew this was not the right thing to do.

This made Qabil even angrier and, not being able to control himself, he attacked and killed Habil. Afterwards, he did not know what to do with his brother's body. Allah sent a crow that started scratching the ground with its feet.

Seeing this, Qabil had the idea to dig a hole in the ground and bury the body. He realised what a terrible thing he had done in listening to the whispers of Shaitan and letting his jealousy and anger drive him to murder his loving brother and bring sadness and shame to his parents.

This was the first murder ever committed. As such, whenever anyone murders someone else, not only is the sin written against the name of the murderer, but also against Qabil's name.

O Allah, shower peace and blessings upon Your Prophet Adam, for every name that You taught him, and for every human soul which is bound by Your covenant.

The Prophet Nuh
(peace be upon him)

Initially, after the death of Adam (peace be upon him), the people were following the Islam he had been sent with, and were worshipping Allah correctly. They looked to his most pious companions for guidance on how to live their lives to please Allah. As time went on, these companions also passed away, so the people had no one to guide and lead them. They feared that they would go astray. Shaitan whispered to them, making it seem like a good idea to make statues of their pious ancestors, whose names were Wadd, Suwa, Yaghuth, Ya'uq, and Nasr.

By looking at the statues and reminding themselves of these pious people, they thought this would encourage them to remember Allah and worship Him correctly. But as time passed, and these people passed away, their descendants forgot the intention behind the making of the statues. Shaitan whispered to them, to make them think their ancestors used to worship these statues as idols, and that by doing so, it would please Allah and bring them good fortune. Therefore, over time, the people started committing *Shirk* (worshipping anything other than Allah). When this had become widespread in the community, Allah sent a Prophet to guide them back to the straight path. This prophet was Nuh (peace be upon him).

Despite preaching to his people for centuries, only a handful of them followed him. The disbelievers called Nuh (peace be upon him) and his followers, liars and threatened them with stoning and expulsion from their homes. They taunted Nuh, asking him to bring about the punishment of Allah if he was speaking the truth. After over 900 years had passed, Allah revealed to Nuh that no-one else would now believe and instructed him to start building the Ark, a huge ship. Allah would soon be sending His punishment on the disbelievers. Seeing Nuh do this in the middle of the desert, they started making even more fun of him.

After the Ark was complete, it was boarded by Nuh (peace be upon him), his family, and the small community of believers. According to Allah's instructions, they also took with them pairs of animals (domesticated and some wild). Then the rain started falling as it had never fallen before, and water started gushing from the surface of the Earth. This continued without stopping until a huge flood, the likes of which was never seen before or since, covered the land. The Prophet Nuh, his followers and animals in the Ark were safe as the boat sailed on waves as big as mountains, but the disbelievers, who had stayed in their houses, climbed onto hills and even on top of mountains, were drowned. This included one of Nuh's own sons, who refused to believe in his father's message.

When Allah's punishment had wiped away the disbelievers, Allah commanded the Earth to swallow its water and the sky to stop its rain. The flood slowly ended and the Ark came to rest on Mount Judi. Allah blessed Nuh (peace be upon him) as he left the Ark and stepped on the now cleansed Earth. The new community that began, did so once more worshipping Allah alone.

O Allah, shower peace and blessings upon Your Prophet Nuh, for every raindrop that has fallen from Your Heavens, for every wave that has risen from Your oceans.

The Prophet Hud
(peace be upon him)

After the time of the Prophet Nuh (peace be upon him) and the great flood, from the descendants of the people saved in the Ark, came the people of Ad. They were a race of people we would consider giants because of how tall and broad they were. This also meant they were extraordinarily strong, and they used this strength to build huge palaces with tall pillars. They lived in a city called Iram. They had found their forefathers committing *Shirk* and worshipping idols and so they continued this tradition. The people of Ad did not believe in an afterlife, and given their pride in their strength, they behaved like tyrants and did whatever they felt like doing.

Allah sent them a Prophet from among themselves called Hud (peace be upon him). He advised them to stop committing Shirk, to stop being proud and arrogant, to stop being extravagant in their buildings as if they were going to live in them forever, and to stop being tyrants. He advised them to think of all the blessings of Allah upon them, and to be grateful for them. The people of Ad rejected their Prophet, calling him a liar since he didn't bring any proof of his claims and so why should they leave their religion and the religion of their forefathers? They told the Prophet Hud they thought it was more likely he was mad, and maybe this was because he had been cursed by one of their Gods. The Prophet Hud challenged them and their Gods, telling them to work against him to try and harm him, he would put his trust in Allah. The people of Ad told Hud that they were not going to listen to him whatever he said, and challenged him that if he was truthful then they awaited the punishment he was promising them.

The people of Ad saw dark clouds forming on the horizon and were happy, thinking this meant it was going to rain, which would be good for their crops. But these weren't rain clouds, and instead hurricane-like winds started that continued non-stop for 8 days. The giant people of Ad, who were so proud of their size and might, were picked up effortlessly by the raging winds and flung here and there, smashing their heads and leaving their dead bodies like the trunks of uprooted trees. The city of Iram, with its huge

palaces and tall pillars was completely destroyed, its ruins a sign for later generations.

O Allah, shower peace and blessings upon Your Prophet Hud, for every gust of wind, from the gentle breeze to the mighty hurricane.

The Prophet Saleh
(peace be upon him)

The people of Thamud lived in a nearby region to the previously destroyed nation of Ad. They were also engaged in idol worship. They were very skilled craftsmen, building their homes inside mountains and cliffs by carving through rock. Allah sent them a Prophet from among themselves called Saleh (peace be upon him). He told them to avoid making the same mistakes as the people of Ad, to learn from their fate and worship Allah alone. He encouraged them to thank Allah for His favours upon them and to behave righteously.

The people of Thamud refused to believe in Saleh as a Prophet (peace be upon him), despite the great respect they had for him before he started calling them towards Islam (submission to the will of Allah). They said that they thought he was bewitched and challenged him to produce a miracle as evidence of his claims, if he was indeed telling the truth. They pointed to a hill and asked Saleh to produce a beautiful, pregnant camel from it. The Prophet Saleh asked them that if Allah was to grant them this miracle, would they believe? They replied that they would. So Saleh raised his hands and prayed to Allah, and the people of Thamud witnessed with their own eyes the splitting of the hill and the emergence of a huge, 10 metre tall, pregnant she-camel from inside it.

Many people kept their promise, believed in Saleh (peace be upon him) as a Prophet and followed him. However, many others, especially the rich and powerful, didn't. The she-camel of Allah was so big that it could eat all the fodder and drink all the water from their wells. The people complained to Saleh, so he set up a system of alternating days so their animals would also get a chance to graze and have water to drink. The she-camel soon gave birth to her baby and produced so much milk every day that all the people of Thamud could drink their fill.

However, the disbelievers could not stand the presence of Allah's she-camel amongst them. It was living proof that Saleh (peace be upon him) and his followers were on the right path and they were too arrogant and stubborn to accept it. So they made a plan to kill her. For this job they chose nine people who were known criminals. They got their weapons and waited alongside the path the she-camel used to walk. As she passed, they viciously and mercilessly attacked her, killing her in front of her calf. The

calf fled from them back to the hill from which its mother had emerged. It cried three times and then disappeared back into the hill.

The disbelievers came to Saleh (peace be upon him) and given what they had just done, challenged him to bring about Allah's punishment if he was truly a Prophet. Saleh told them that they only had three days to enjoy themselves before the punishment of Allah was coming. Now it mattered not what they did, there was no way to stop it. This frightened the disbelievers who hid in their homes, perhaps hoping that sheltering inside mountains and cliffs would save them from whatever was going to happen. However, the worst of the disbelievers made further plans to kill Saleh. But while they were making their plan, Allah also had a plan. They did not know Allah's plan, but Allah knew their plan. Allah told Saleh to leave with the people who followed him. At the end of the three days the disbelievers heard an unimaginably horrible, thundering scream. Everyone who heard it was instantly killed, cowering in their stone houses.

O Allah, shower peace and blessings upon Your Prophet Saleh, for every mountain, for every cliff, for every boulder, for every rock, for every stone, for every pebble, and for every grain of sand.

The Prophet Ibrahim
(peace be upon him)

Ibrahim (peace be upon him) was chosen as a Prophet of Allah from childhood. He lived with a relative called Azar, an idol maker. His people believed the bright stars in the sky were their Gods, and worshipped idols as a way to please these Gods and gain their favour. One day, Ibrahim asked Azar why he worshipped things that could not see or hear him, and could not help him in any way? He told him that this is like worshipping Shaitan and will result in Allah's punishment. But Azar wouldn't listen to him, instead becoming angry because this child was questioning his religion and rejecting his Gods. He told Ibrahim that if he didn't stop, he would stone him.

On another occasion, Ibrahim (peace be upon him) went with his people up on the mountain. As night fell, he looked at the brightest star and said, *"This is my Lord."* But then the star disappeared, and the Moon appeared, which was larger and more beautiful. So Ibrahim said, *"This is my Lord."* But then as morning drew close, the light of the Moon faded, and the Sun rose. Ibrahim said, *"This is my Lord, this is greater."* But then as night approached, the Sun set again. He told his people he could not worship these things, which were all creations of Allah, when he could worship the Creator. All these other things came and went, appeared and disappeared, were finite no matter how great they seemed, but the Creator was eternal, infinite, always present and could never disappear.

The day of the big festival arrived, but Ibrahim (peace be upon him) made an excuse that he was unwell and stayed behind. He entered the temple with an axe. In the temple were all the biggest idols, beautifully decorated for the festival and with lots of delicious foods put in front of them. Ibrahim asked the idols why they weren't eating, he asked them why they weren't replying to him? He smashed all of them to pieces with his axe, which he hung around the neck of the biggest idol and left.

When the people returned to the temple, they were shocked to find all their idols destroyed. They could not imagine who would do such a thing, but then remembered that there was one young man who often spoke out against their idols. So they called Ibrahim (peace be upon

him) and asked him if he had done this. He replied that it must have been the biggest idol, the only one that wasn't smashed and had the axe next to him. He told them to ask it what had happened. They replied that obviously the idol could not speak. So Ibrahim replied by questioning them again, about why they worshipped things that couldn't speak, hear or see? Why they worshipped completely life-less things that couldn't move even to defend themselves, let alone help something else? How did worshipping these things instead of Allah make any sense?

The people knew Ibrahim (peace be upon him) was speaking the truth, but out of stubbornness and arro-gance they could not bring themselves to admit it and change their ways. Having no reply, they became angry with Ibrahim for humiliating them and decided to punish him. They started gathering wood to build the biggest fire the world has ever seen. From far and wide, a mountain of wood was collected and when they lit it on fire, no-one could stand close to it because of the searing heat. From a distance it seemed as if the flames were touching the sky and birds would not fly over the raging fire. But the people now faced a problem, how could they throw Ibrahim into the fire when they couldn't even get close to it? Shaitan provided them with the solution, to build a new invention not previously seen in the world – the catapult. Ibrahim was chained, loaded into the catapult, and hurled into the blazing inferno.

Despite facing what looked like a certain and very painful death, the Prophet Ibrahim (peace be upon him) had complete faith in Allah and whatever plan his Creator had for him. While hurtling through the air, the Archangel Jibra'il (peace be upon him) came to him and asked him if he wanted help. Ibrahim replied that he did not need any help, because he knew that only what Allah wills was going to happen, and he was happy to accept that. He prayed, *"Hasbun'Allahu wa ni'mal wakeel (Allah is sufficient for us and he is the best disposer of our affairs)."* Allah ordered the fire to become cool and safe for Ibrahim. The people watching couldn't believe their eyes as they witnessed a miracle. Ibrahim was walking about in the middle of the inferno. After 40-50 days, the Prophet Ibrahim walked out of the still burning fire, completely unhurt.

Ibrahim and Namrud

Around this time a famine had struck, and food and water were scarce. The people had to go to the court of the king of the ancient city of Babylon to request provisions. This king was called Namrud, who had reigned his vast kingdom for hundreds of years, and claimed he was a God. Ibrahim (peace be upon him) also went to Namrud, who asked him what was special about the God he was asking everyone to worship. The Prophet told him that God was the giver and taker of life. In response to this Namrud had his guards bring in a prisoner who was due to

be executed, and a person who just happened to be walking past the palace. He ordered the prisoner to be set free
and the execution of the free person. Then, turning to Ibrahim he boasted that he could also give life and death. In
reply, Ibrahim said that God is the one who raises the Sun
from the East and makes it set in the West – if Namrud was
God, then he should be able to make it rise from the West.
Namrud did not have an answer to this and was humiliated
in front of his court. So he told Ibrahim that he did not have
any food or water to give him, instead he should ask for it
from his God.

Turned away empty handed, as he neared home,
Ibrahim (peace be upon him) filled his sacks with sand.
He did this to make his wife, Sarah (may Allah be pleased
with her), think that he had been given provisions, and not
to worry. When he arrived home, he put the sacks to one

side and, being tired from the journey, fell asleep. Sarah opened the sacks and found them full of food, which she prepared for her husband. When Ibrahim awoke, he saw all the food and asked his wife where it had come from. When she replied that it was from the sacks that he had brought back with him, he realised Allah had provided for them.

In contrast to this, Allah sent an Angel in human form to Namrud, who asked him to believe in Allah and give up his claim of godhood. Namrud refused. He was offered two further chances but refused again and again. The Angel then challenged him, that the time for war had come. Namrud gathered his huge armies but against them Allah sent an army of mosquitoes that blocked out the Sun. The mosquitoes descended upon the terrified human soldiers and sucked their bodies dry of blood. Namrud had a special punishment reserved for him. A mosquito flew up his nose and into his skull. When it would crawl across the surface of his brain he couldn't bear the feeling, the itching, the pain, and would smash his head against the wall or ask people to beat his head with sticks. Finally, in this tortured state, this king who claimed he was a God, died a humiliating death.

Hajar

Ibrahim (peace be upon him) and his wife, Sarah (may Allah be pleased with her) migrated. On their travels, they passed a land where a tyrant king lived who had

a reputation for kidnapping beautiful women. The king's spies told him that a traveller had entered his lands and a most beautiful woman was with him. They kidnapped Sarah and brought her to the king. Ibrahim knew there was nothing he could do to stop the king, so he prayed to Allah for Him to keep Sarah safe. In the meantime, the king tried to grab hold of Sarah, but she also prayed to Allah and the king's body became paralysed. He asked her to release him, and she prayed to Allah to make him well again. However, when he could move, he again tried to grab hold of her. But again, she prayed to Allah, and he became paralysed. He again asked her to release him. This happened three or four times after which he became scared and shouted at his guards for bringing him a witch or a devil. He sent her back to Ibrahim and gave her one of his slaves called Hajar (may Allah be pleased with them both).

Ibrahim (peace be upon him) and Sarah (may Allah be pleased with her) had not been able to have children together and they were getting old, so Sarah asked Ibrahim to marry her maid, Hajar (may Allah be pleased with her). They had a baby boy together called Ismail (peace be upon him). Soon afterwards, Allah commanded His Prophet Ibrahim to leave Hajar and Ismail in the middle of the baking, lifeless desert. This would normally mean certain death. Very soon, the baby started crying because he was hot and thirsty so Hajar ran up one hill to see if there was any water around or any travellers she could ask for help. Seeing no-one and wanting to check on her baby, she ran back down before running up the other hill to do the same. She did this seven times, and these hills are called Safa and Marwa. After this, in some stories it says the baby rubbed his heel on the ground while crying; in others it says the Archangel Jibra'il (peace be upon him) hit the ground with his wing. Either way, the result was the appearance of a water spring in the middle of the desert. Seeing how much water was gushing out, Hajar said 'ZamZam' – meaning 'Stop! Stop!' Over time, travellers passing through the desert created a settlement near this new water source.

Ismail and Ishaq

It would be nearly 10 years before Ibrahim went back to visit Hajar and Ismail (peace be upon them all). But soon afterwards he had a dream in which he was sac-

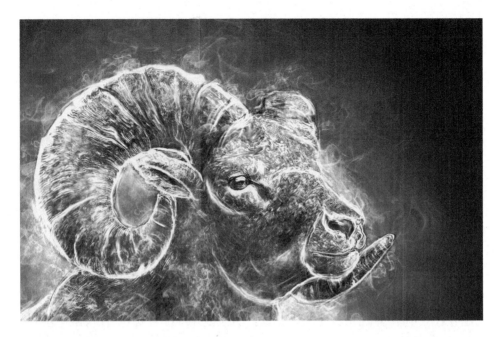

rificing his son. Ibrahim knew that the dreams of Prophets are special, they are a form of Revelation from Allah. He told Ismail what he had seen in his dream, to which his son replied that he should do as Allah had commanded. On their way, Shaitan appeared to each of them in turn, father, mother and son, desperate to stop them obeying Allah in this most difficult test. But the Shaitan failed each time, more important than their love for each other was their desire to please Allah – they could not disobey Him.

In some stories it says Ibrahim laid Ismail face down so he wouldn't see the face of his son while trying to sacrifice him (peace be upon them both). In other stories it says he wore a blindfold. Either way, he went ahead with the sacrifice, running the sharp knife over the neck of his son but the knife would not cut. He tried again, but again, the knife would not cut. When he tried a third time, the knife

cut, and the sacrifice was done. However, when Ibrahim removed his blindfold or looked down, he was surprised to see that he had sacrificed a ram and Ismail was standing unhurt next to him. Allah had told the knife to become blunt when Ibrahim was running it across Ismail's neck, and told Jibra'il (peace be upon him) to take a ram from Paradise and replace Ismail with it. Allah told Ibrahim he had passed the test and his sacrifice had been accepted.

After some time had passed, Allah told Ibrahim (peace be upon him) to build the Ka'bah – the first house of worship. He did this with his son, Ismail (peace be upon him) upon holy land that was chosen from when the Earth was created. The Ka'bah of the humans lies directly below the Ka'bah of the Angels on the seventh Heaven, which is visited by 70,000 Angels every day. To help them build the Ka'bah, when the walls had gotten too high, Ibrahim stood on a special stone Allah sent from the Heavens. This would move and grow larger allowing them to complete building the high walls of the Ka'bah. While he was standing on it the stone became soft, so his footprints were left on it. In one of the corners of the Ka'bah is another stone from Heaven, called *al-Hajar'al-Aswad* (the Black Stone). This was originally pure white in colour, but over centuries has become black as it has absorbed the sins of people who touch it and kiss it. These two stones are two jewels from Paradise but Allah has hidden their light, otherwise they would have brightened the whole Earth.

Ibrahim (peace be upon him) once prayed to Allah to show him how He gave life to the dead. This was not because he had any doubt about Allah's ability to do this, but to see it with his own eyes. Allah granted the request of His friend[iv]. He told Ibrahim to take four birds, cut them into pieces and mix all the pieces together. Then, divide them into piles and put one pile on the top of four nearby mountains and call to them. When Ibrahim did this, the body parts of each bird started separating, flying and joining to each other until the four birds stood on the four mountain tops, before flying to Ibrahim.

Ibrahim (peace be upon him) and Sarah (may Allah be pleased with her) had become quite old, beyond the age people can normally have children. However, one day they were visited by Angels who told them Allah was going to bless them with a son called Ishaq, who would go on to have a son called Yaqub (peace be upon them both).

---

iv   One of Ibrahim's titles was Khalil'Allah – friend of Allah.

O Allah, shower peace and blessings upon Your Prophets Ibrahim, Ismail and Ishaq, for every drop of ZamZam, for every kiss of al-Hajar'al-Aswad, for every circumambulation of the Ka'bah, and for every hair of every Qurbani.

The Prophet Lut
(peace be upon him)

The Prophet Lut was Ibrahim's nephew (peace be upon them both). He settled in the city of Sodom. The people of Sodom were committing a sin no-one before them had practiced. The men would get married to other men rather than women. Lut tried to warn them that this was not according to the purpose Allah had created men and women for, that this was a major sin that would bring Allah's anger upon them. However, no-one was willing to listen to him. They mocked him and his family for thinking they were so clean and pure and threatened to expel them from the city.

Lut (peace be upon him) continued to patiently preach to his people but not a single person followed him. Finally, the time came when Allah sent His punishment.

Three Angels, Jibra'il, Mika'il, and Israfil (peace be upon them all), came in the form of handsome young men. They went to Lut's house as travellers and he gave them a place to stay overnight. However, knowing the behaviour of the people of Sodom, the Prophet was very distressed and felt fearful for his guests. Lut's wife was a hypocrite, and she secretly told people that in her house were three beautiful male travellers. The people came rushing to Lut's house and surrounded it, demanding that he turn his guests over to them so they could kidnap them.

The Prophet's worst fear had come true. From behind his closed door he desperately tried preaching to his people one more time. He again told them to go to their wives, or for those who were not married, to look for women in the community, instead of other men. He told them to fear Allah and to leave his guests alone. The people had no interest in listening to what Lut (peace be upon him) had to say and refused to leave without getting what they came for.

The guests revealed to Lut (peace be upon him) that they were Angels, that the punishment of Allah had arrived and he need not fear. Jibra'il (peace be upon him) stepped outside the house and struck the peoples' faces with his wing. This caused their eyes to disappear, leaving them completely blind. The Angels told Lut to leave with his family and not to look back.

As the dawn came the Angels got to work. A thunderous sound was heard as a huge earthquake shook the entire city and caused a tremendous volcanic eruption. Burning rocks rained down upon the destroyed city. The wife of Lut (peace be upon him) was destined to be punished with the disbelievers, and so she could not stop herself from looking back when she heard the punishment of Allah destroying the city. As she did so, a burning rock fell from the sky and killed her. Where the city of Sodom once was is now the Dead Sea. On all the land of the Earth, it is the deepest part. Its water is so salty (nearly 10 times more than the ocean) that nothing lives in the water, giving it its name.

O Allah, shower peace and blessings upon Your Prophet Lut, for every husband and wife, and the depth of the love that You place in their hearts.

The Prophet Shoaib
(peace be upon him)

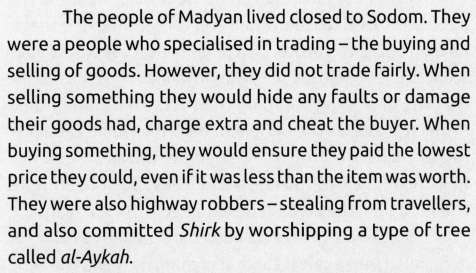

The people of Madyan lived closed to Sodom. They were a people who specialised in trading – the buying and selling of goods. However, they did not trade fairly. When selling something they would hide any faults or damage their goods had, charge extra and cheat the buyer. When buying something, they would ensure they paid the lowest price they could, even if it was less than the item was worth. They were also highway robbers – stealing from travellers, and also committed *Shirk* by worshipping a type of tree called *al-Aykah*.

Allah sent to them a Prophet from among themselves called Shoaib (peace be upon him). He preached to them to worship and thank Allah for the wealth they had been given, and not to be ungrateful and greedy by cheating and stealing from people. It would be better for them to be satisfied with having less but earning it in a *Halal* way than using *Haram* means to try and get as much as they could, because the *Haram* means would earn the anger of Allah.

The people of Madyan argued with their Prophet, that why should they leave the religion of their forefathers and why shouldn't they do whatever they want with their own money? Shoaib (peace be upon him) continued preaching to them, to change their ways otherwise Allah's punishment would descend on them as it had on the people of Nuh, Hud, Saleh and Lut (peace be upon them all).

But his preaching fell on deaf ears, most of the people refused to follow him and threatened him that if he didn't have the protection of his tribe, they would have stoned him. Shoaib (peace be upon him) found it incredible that the only thing stopping them from murdering their Prophet was that the people of his tribe would retaliate, rather than fear of Allah. The people further threatened him and his few followers, that if they did not return to their religion, they would be expelled from Madyan.

So, Shoaib (peace be upon him) prayed to Allah for help. Allah sent against them scorching heat and the wind stopped blowing. They could not find relief in their homes or in the shade. Their wealth could not help them. After seven days the sky darkened but instead of wind and rain, an earthquake happened with a thunderous blast that left them lifeless in their homes.

O Allah, shower peace and blessings upon Your Prophet Shoaib, for every coin of every currency spent in Your way and to the extent of Your reward.

The Prophet Yusuf
(peace be upon him)

Ibrahim and Sarah had a son called Ishaq, who had a son call Yaqub. Yaqub had 12 sons and the second youngest was called Yusuf. Ibrahim, Ishaq, Yaqub and Yusuf were all Prophets of Allah (peace be upon them all). Yusuf was the favourite of his father. When he was a young child he had a dream in which he saw the Sun, the Moon and 11 stars, and they were all bowing to him. He told this dream to his father, Yaqub, who told him not to tell his brothers since it would make them feel even more jealous of him. His father understood that this was a special dream which meant his son was going to be someone very important.

Yusuf's older brothers were so jealous of the love and attention they felt their father gave him, that they

made a plan to kill him. They thought that if Yusuf (peace be upon him) was no longer with them, their father would love them more. And after getting rid of Yusuf, they could repent to Allah and be good people. One of the brothers said that instead of killing him, they should throw him into a well, so a passing caravan might rescue him and take him with them. So the brothers went to Yaqub (peace be upon him) and asked him to allow them to take Yusuf with them when they next went out. They pretended they were asking because they felt sorry for Yusuf not being allowed to play with his brothers. They promised they would take care of him. Yaqub was reluctant, he didn't want Yusuf to leave his side and told them he was worried Yusuf may come to some harm while with them, such as a wolf attacking him. They reassured their father, that with so many of them, how could a wolf attack Yusuf? Yaqub gave in, and let them take him.

The brothers put their plan into action and, after having travelled some distance from home, threw Yusuf (peace be upon him) into a well. At that moment, Allah told Yusuf that there will come a time when he shall remind them of what they did to him, but they will not be able to recognise him. Yusuf's brothers spread some animal blood on his shirt and waited until night to return home. They cried fake tears and told Yaqub (peace be upon him) that they had been racing. While distracted, a wolf had come and eaten Yusuf. Yaqub knew they were lying but he also knew this must be the will of Allah. He knew that

everything Allah does contains good for the believer, so he resorted to being patient and trusting in Allah's plan.

Yusuf in Egypt

After some time, a caravan passed by and stopped to get water from the well. However, when they lifted out the bucket they were shocked to see a small boy sitting in it. They travelled on to Egypt, where they sold Yusuf (peace be upon him) as a slave. He was bought by one of the king's ministers (Aziz), who told his wife, Zulaykha to take care of Yusuf and that they might even adopt him as a son. So Yusuf, while still a young child, went from being at home with his loving father to thrown into a well and left to die by his own brothers, then sold as a slave, but bought by someone rich and powerful who wanted to treat him kindly.

As Yusuf (peace be upon him) grew up in Aziz's household, Allah blessed him with exceptional beauty and wisdom. Over time, Zulaykha started developing feelings for him. One day she called him into a room and shut all the doors. She could not control herself and tried to seduce him. Yusuf prayed to Allah for help, to be able to control himself and not commit a major sin. He reminded Zulaykha that her husband, who was his master, was a good man and had taken good care of him. How could they betray him? But Zulaykha would not listen, and as Yusuf ran to the door

to escape from her, she ran after him, grabbing the back of his shirt and accidentally tearing it.

Just as they reached the door, it opened and there stood Aziz. Knowing she was the one who had done wrong, Zulaykha immediately accused Yusuf (peace be upon him) of trying to seduce her and asked her husband to punish him. Yusuf spoke the truth and told Aziz that his wife was lying. One of his advisors told him to check Yusuf's shirt to know who was telling the truth. If it was ripped from the front then he had attacked her and she was trying to save herself, but if it was ripped from the back then he was running from her and she was trying to catch him. When they checked Yusuf's shirt, it was ripped from the back. Aziz told his wife off for not only trying to seduce Yusuf, but then lying about it and accusing him. He told Yusuf not to tell anyone about this and told Zulaykha to repent to Allah.

However, rumours spread in the city and other women started gossiping how the minister's wife had fallen in love with her slave. Zulaykha came up with a plan to put an end to the rumours. She invited the women to her house and gave them apples to eat and knives to cut them. But before they could start eating, she called Yusuf (peace be upon him) into the room. When the women saw Yusuf, and how beautiful he was, they were mesmerised. Instead of cutting the apples, they accidentally cut their hands and didn't even notice. They remarked that this can't be a man, he must be an Angel.

   The women stopped looking down on Zulaykha for having fallen in love with her slave and now encouraged her to seduce him, which she tried to do again. She threatened him that if he did not give in she would have him thrown into prison. Yusuf (peace be upon him) prayed to Allah to save him again, because he would prefer prison to betraying his master and disobeying Allah. Allah accepted his prayer and saved him. Aziz decided that even though Yusuf was innocent, it would be better to send him to prison to stop people talking and save the reputation of his household.

Interpreting dreams

Yusuf (peace be upon him) spent his time in prison worshipping Allah and teaching the other prisoners about Allah and the religion of his forefathers, Yaqub, Ishaq, and Ibrahim (peace be upon them all). One of the special wisdoms Allah had granted Yusuf was the ability to interpret dreams. One day two prisoners came to him with their dreams wanting to know the meaning of them. One was the king's cupbearer, and he saw a dream that he was pressing grapes into the king's cup. The other was the king's baker, and he saw himself carrying a basket of bread on his head which wild birds were eating from. Yusuf told the cup-bearer that he would be released from prison and return to work for the king, and he told the baker that

unfortunately his dream meant he would be executed. Indeed, things happened just as Yusuf had prophesised.

Before leaving prison, Yusuf (peace be upon him) had asked the cup-bearer to mention his name to the king. However, he forgot to do this until, some years later, the king asked his advisors to explain to him the meaning of a strange dream he had seen. Seven fat cows were being eaten by seven thin cows, and he had seen seven green ears of corn and seven shrivelled up ears of corn. None of the advisors could explain the dream but when the cup-bearer heard it, he remembered Yusuf. He told the king there was a wise man in prison who could help. Finding Yusuf, he told him the king's dream. Yusuf explained this meant there were going to be seven years when the crops would grow well and there would be an excess of food, but this would be followed by seven years of famine. He advised that to stop the people from starving during the seven years of famine, all the excess food grown during the first seven years would need to be carefully stored and not wasted.

When the cup-bearer returned to the king and told him the interpretation of his dream, the king was impressed and wanted to meet Yusuf (peace be upon him). But Yusuf first asked him to find out what had happened with the women who cut their hands. The king questioned Zulaykha and the women. They admitted that Yusuf was innocent. Zulaykha admitted she was the one who had tried to seduce him, he had always behaved honourably and told

the truth. Now that the truth had come out and everyone knew that Yusuf was innocent and wrongly imprisoned, he met with the king. The king wanted to make Yusuf one of his advisors so Yusuf asked to be put in charge of the treasury. Yusuf had gone from growing up in the house of Aziz and Zulaykha to spending years in prison for something he did not do, to working directly for the king as a minister himself.

The king's minister

Just as Yusuf (peace be upon him) has prophesised from the king's dreams, for seven years there was good weather and the crops grew well, so the storehouses were overflowing. Then the weather changed and famine struck. People from all over the kingdom would come to the king's court, where Yusuf was in charge of distributing food in exchange for money or goods. Yusuf's family was also affected by the famine and so his brothers travelled to Egypt. Yusuf recognised them but they did not recognise him – not in their wildest dreams could they imagine that the brother they had thrown down a well as a small child was now sitting before them as a high minister in charge of all the food in the kingdom. Yusuf asked them about their circumstances and they told him where they were from, that they were 12 brothers in total but one had disappeared and the youngest, Binyamin, was at home with their father. Yusuf gave them the food they had come to

collect but also told them to bring their youngest brother with them the next time they came, otherwise they would not get any more food. Before they left, Yusuf told his servants to secretly put the money they had paid for the food back into their bags.

When the brothers returned home they went to their father and told him that next time they would have to take Binyamin with them otherwise the minister would not give them any more food. Yaqub (peace be upon him) asked them, *"Shall I trust him with you just as I trusted you with Yusuf?"* When the brothers unpacked the food they had bought, they were shocked to also find the money they had paid. So, they went back to their father and told him what they had discovered. This meant they could go back and get even more food for their family, but they could only do that if he let Binyamin go with them. Yaqub reluc-

tantly agreed after making them take an oath in Allah's name that unless it was beyond their control, they would bring Binyamin back to him.

When the brothers returned to Egypt, Yusuf (peace be upon him) took Binyamin to one side and revealed his true identity. Binyamin told Yusuf about how their brothers were mistreating him because they were jealous of how much Yaqub (peace be upon him) loved him. Yusuf made a plan of how to keep Binyamin in Egypt with him and told his servants to put something into their luggage. As they were leaving, a messenger stopped them accusing someone in the party of being a thief. The brothers asked what was missing and were told it was the king's drinking cup. They protested their innocence saying they had not come here with bad intentions. They were asked that if one of them turned out to be the thief, what should the punishment be? They replied that the thief should be kept as a slave.

When their luggage was searched, the cup was found in Binyamin's bag. The brothers were shocked and begged Yusuf (peace be upon him) not to stop Binyamin from going home with them, knowing the effect this would have on their father. They even asked him to keep one of them instead but Yusuf refused, saying that would be unjust, it must be the thief who is punished. When they had lost all hope of taking Binyamin back with them, the oldest brother reminded everyone of the promise they had made their father and said he would stay in Egypt until

he could return home with Binyamin. He told his brothers to go back home and tell Yaqub (peace be upon him) what had happened.

When Yaqub (peace be upon him) heard the news he did not believe Binyamin would have stolen the cup. He thought his sons had betrayed him again. The pain of losing Yusuf (peace be upon him) was once again reawakened in his heart, and he withdrew from his family. Yaqub cried so much and for so long that he became blind. However, he did not lose hope that Allah would one day return his sons to him. He knew this because Yusuf's dream, of the Sun, Moon and stars bowing to him, hadn't yet come true.

Yusuf's dream

When the food they had bought ran out, the brothers travelled back to Egypt. They pleaded with Yusuf (peace be upon him) to be charitable, to give them food for their family even though they had run out of money and goods to trade for it. When Yusuf saw the difficulty his family was in, he could bear it no longer and asked them directly if they remembered what they had done with Yusuf? Asked this strange question, the brothers finally looked closely at the minister and for the first time thought about whether they recognised him. They were shocked at what they saw, and asked him if he was their brother, Yusuf. Yusuf revealed who he was, and that their brother, Binyamin was also safe with him. He told them that Allah had been gen-

erous to him and his younger brother because they had been patient and remembered Allah during the hardships they had gone through.

The brothers were already feeling guilty for what they had done to Yusuf (peace be upon him), given the grief it had caused their father, but now they also realised that Allah had indeed chosen Yusuf over them. They confessed their fault to Yusuf, but instead of being angry or punishing them (which he could easily do now he was a powerful minister to the king), Yusuf forgave them and asked Allah to forgive them. Yusuf gave them his shirt and told them to take it home to their father, Yaqub (peace be upon him), and place it on his eyes. He told them to bring their whole family back to Egypt with them.

The brothers hurried back home. While they were still on the way, Yaqub (peace be upon him) told the people

around him that he could smell the beautiful scent of his son, Yusuf (peace be upon him), and his heart became hopeful. When the caravan arrived and his sons placed Yusuf's shirt upon their father's eyes, a miracle of Allah occurred and he could see again. They told him the good news and Yaqub reminded them, *"Did I not tell you I have knowledge from Allah that you do not have?"* His sons admitted what they had done and asked their father to forgive them and to pray for Allah to forgive them, which he did. The whole family then travelled to Egypt to live there, and Yusuf and Binyamin were finally reunited with their parents. Out of honour and respect, Yusuf's parents and brothers bowed down to him. This was finally the fulfilment of his childhood dream.

O Allah, shower peace and blessings upon Your Prophets Yaqub and Yusuf, for every ray of the Sun, for every beam of the Moon, for every star in the sky.

The Prophet Ayyub
(peace be upon him)

One of Prophet Lut's daughters had a son called Ayyub, who was also a Prophet of Allah (peace be upon them both). Allah had blessed Ayyub with lots of money, land, and animals. As a Prophet, he would not only guide people to worship Allah but also help the poor and needy with everything he had. Apart from his wealth, he also had a loving wife and many children, and good health despite reaching the age of 70. But in his old age Allah tested him by taking away these blessings.

One after another, calamity struck. Ayyub's animals died and he made business losses which ended up in him losing his money and land. Then, an accident happened in which all his children died. Allah even tested Ayyub (peace be upon him) by taking away his good health. He developed diseases that affected every part of his body except his intellect and his speech. The people of the town he lived in, including his friends and relatives, who used to love and respect him, didn't want anything to do with him. In fact, they didn't even come close to him because they were worried they might catch his diseases. So he was forced to leave his home and live outside the town, alone, in the place where everybody threw their rubbish.

The only person who stayed with him was his wife, who remembered how well he had taken care of her his whole life and that he was a Prophet of Allah (peace be upon him). So she still loved and supported him as best as she could during this most difficult test. But to be able to take care of him, even to buy food to eat, she had to earn money by working. But even this was difficult to do because people knew she was the wife of Ayyub and was still helping him. So they didn't want to give her a job where she was close to other people in case she had the same diseases her husband did. When she couldn't find any work, she even ended up selling her hair.

Ayyub (peace be upon him) and his wife suffered for many years. But during all this time he remained patient and continued worshipping Allah just as much as he had always done. Once his wife asked him why he didn't pray to Allah to relieve him from this suffering. But Ayyub answered that Allah had granted him good health for 70 years, so shouldn't he bear patiently with poor health for 70 years? This shows how, even during this most difficult test, having lost his wealth, his family, his respect, his health, he remained grateful to Allah for all He had given him and continued to bless him with.

Finally, when the disease started affecting his ability to worship Allah, Ayyub (peace be upon him) prayed for relief from his suffering, since he could bear to lose all the other blessings of Allah, but not the ability to remember his Creator. Allah told him to strike the ground with his foot. Upon doing so a spring of water emerged. Allah told him to bathe himself in this water and drink from it. Ayyub was cured of all internal and external diseases. Not only this, but he started to look more beautiful and became more energetic, as if he was a younger man. When his wife came home, at first she did not recognise him and asked where her husband was? He explained to her what had happened. Allah also returned his wealth to him. So much so, that it even began to rain down golden locusts on him. His family was also returned. Some stories say his children were brought back to life, others say that he was given more children and in the afterlife, they will all be together.

O Allah, shower peace and blessings upon Your Prophet Ayyub, for every ounce of patience within the hearts of Your slaves and every word of gratitude on the tongues of Your slaves.

The Prophet Yunus
(peace be upon him)

The Prophet Yunus (peace be upon him) was sent to the people of Nineveh. He preached to them for many years, to leave their sinful ways, to stop committing *Shirk*, to worship Allah as He has instructed them to, which would bring them benefit in this life and the next. However, as with previous Prophets, the people refused to believe in his Prophethood or to listen to what he had to say. Finally, believing he had done everything he could to call his people to the right path, Yunus threatened them that Allah's punishment would descend upon them in three days, and left Nineveh. Once Yunus had left, the people of Nineveh became worried. They began to believe that Yunus truly was a Prophet of Allah and Allah's punishment would descend upon them in three days. They remembered stories of what had happened to the people of previous Prophets, who had been utterly destroyed.

Meanwhile, Yunus (peace be upon him) had boarded a ship. Initially the weather was good but once they were out over the open ocean, dark clouds gathered and huge waves started rocking the ship this way and that. The passengers knew that nothing happens without the will of Allah, and given how suddenly the weather had turned, they thought there must be someone on board the ship who had displeased Allah. They thought of how they could determine who this person was to throw them overboard and came up with a plan for all the passengers to write their names on pieces of paper, and the name that was picked out would be the culprit. But when they did this, the name they picked was Yunus'. The passengers believed Yunus to be the most pious of them all, and so couldn't believe this was the right result. So they drew lots again, but again Yunus' name was chosen. They again believed this to be the wrong result, and so drew lots a third time, and yet again, Yunus' name was chosen.

Yunus (peace be upon him) realised he had made a mistake in leaving his people without waiting for Allah's command, that he had been impatient. This was the will of Allah and so he told the passengers not to worry, that he was the one who needed to leave the ship. Once Yunus was thrown into the ocean the weather calmed down, but suddenly, a huge whale rose up from the depths and swallowed him whole. Meanwhile, the people of Nineveh were desperate to try and avoid the punishment of Allah. Every man, woman and child left the city and entered the desert, and even took their animals with them. They begged and cried in front of Allah, seeking repentance for their sins, for the way they had treated their Prophet. This was the only time in history that an entire people had believed in their Prophet, and Allah forgave them.

Yunus (peace be upon him) was in complete darkness in the belly of the whale, which had descended back into the depths of the ocean. Yunus was sure he was going to die here, but all he was concerned with was for Allah to forgive him. So he prayed in the depths of the ocean, in the belly of the whale, in complete darkness, *"There is no one worthy of worship except for You. Glory be to You! Truly, I have been from the wrongdoers."* He thanked Allah for allowing him to worship Him in a place that no-one else had ever done so. The Angels said to Allah that they recognised the voice that was praising Him, but they did not recognise the place it was coming from. Allah told them it was His slave, Yunus, worshipping Him in the belly of a whale in the depths of the ocean. The Angels asked if this was the same Yunus from whom good deeds ascended day and night? Allah said it was. So the Angels prayed to Allah for his forgiveness as well.

Allah had already forgiven his Prophet (peace be upon him), and commanded the whale to rise from the depths of the ocean and throw Yunus out onto a barren shore under the burning Sun. Having spent so many days

inside the belly of the whale, Yunus' body was weak and sick. Allah caused a marrow plant to grow on the shore, its big leaves providing him with shade and its fruit providing him with food, until he had regained his health. Eventually, Allah reunited the people of Nineveh with their Prophet. In the Qur'an, Allah calls Yunus *'Dhu'al-Noon'* – the companion of the fish.

O Allah, shower peace and blessings upon Your Prophet Yunus, for every mistake You have overlooked, for every moment of heedlessness You have ignored, for every tear shed seeking Your forgiveness, and for every slave You have enveloped in Your mercy.

The Prophet Musa
(peace be upon him)

Many generations after Yusuf (peace be upon him), Egypt was ruled by a Pharaoh. The Egyptians worshipped many Gods and also believed Pharaoh was a God. The Israelites (12 tribes descended from the 12 sons of the Prophet Yaqub – peace be upon him) also lived in Egypt, but they were treated like slaves by the Egyptians and had no rights. Pharaoh once had a dream, in which he saw a fire coming from the direction of *Bait'al-Maqdis* (Jerusalem) that destroyed all the Egyptians and their houses, but left the Israelites. When he awoke, he gathered his advisers, priests, sorcerers and soothsayers and asked their advice on what this strange dream meant. They told him a boy would be born to the Israelites who would destroy his kingdom. This scared the Pharaoh and so he ordered for every male baby born to the Israelites to be killed.

Egyptian soldiers and midwives would spy on the Israelites, and those who were pregnant were regularly visited so when they gave birth, it could be checked if the baby was a boy or girl. However, after years of this dreadful torment the Egyptian people became worried. They complained to their rulers that if this policy wasn't changed, in future there wouldn't be enough Israelite slaves and they would have to do their own work. So the Pharaoh changed his policy so baby boys born to the Israelites would only be killed every other year, allowing half of them to live.

A woman among the Israelites, who already had a daughter, had a son in the year baby boys were being allowed to live. She named this baby Haroon (peace be upon him). Then, she became pregnant, but this time the baby would be born in the year baby boys were being killed. Throughout the pregnancy she was terrified she would have another son, and the Egyptian soldiers would kill him. However, as the pregnancy progressed her tummy did not grow that much and so the Egyptian spies weren't sure if she was pregnant or not. When she gave birth, it was a baby boy and she named him Musa (peace be upon him). Musa's mother didn't know what to do, and she was worried the Egyptian soldiers might check in on her at any time and find him. Allah inspired her to put Musa in a basket and then put the basket into the Nile river, which flowed next to her house. Allah inspired her that she shouldn't feel sad or afraid for him, Allah would protect him and return him to her, because he was due to be a Prophet.

Raised by Pharaoh

But after doing this, Musa's mother was so distressed thinking about her baby that she asked her daughter to follow the basket. The Nile carried the basket all the way to the Pharaoh's palace, which was also situated on the banks of the great river. When the basket was brought to Asiyah, the wife of the Pharaoh, she opened it and was amazed to find a beautiful baby boy inside. The Pharaoh and his wife had not been able to have any children, and so Asiyah took the baby to her husband. She pleaded with him to let her keep the baby, that they could adopt him as a son, and eventually he agreed. However, when they tried to find a woman to breastfeed him, the baby refused to feed. They tried many different women but none of them could get Musa (peace be upon him) to take their milk. His sister told them that she could find a woman who would be able to feed him and took them to her house without revealing who she was. In this way, Musa's mother was reunited with her son. When Asiyah saw that the baby was finally feeding, she arranged for Musa to be brought to his mother every day. In this way he grew up in front of his mother's eyes, and despite being an Israelite, he was not a slave like his people or treated badly by the Egyptians because everyone knew he was the adopted son of the Pharaoh.

As Musa (peace be upon him) grew up, Allah blessed him with great strength. One day, when he was walking through the streets of Egypt as a young man, he saw an Egyptian arguing with an Israelite slave. The slave saw Musa and asked him for help. Musa felt it was his duty to help his less fortunate, Israelite brother, and so took his side over the Egyptian. In doing so, he punched the Egyptian and with that single punch, killed him. Musa was shocked, he had not meant to do this. He immediately asked Allah for forgiveness. However, he now felt scared someone would find out what he had done, and the Pharaoh would punish him.

The next day, as he was walking through the city, he came across the same Israelite slave, this time arguing

with a different Egyptian man. When the slave saw Musa (peace be upon him), he again asked him for help. However, Musa now realised that he was a troublemaker who must get into fights and arguments all the time. When he refused to help him, siding with the Egyptian, the Israelite slave became angry and asked if Musa would kill him today like he killed the Egyptian yesterday. News reached Pharaoh that Musa was the one who killed the Egyptian, and he sent out his soldiers and spies to capture him. But before they could catch him, someone told Musa that he better leave Egypt, otherwise, if they caught him, he would be executed.

Meeting Shoaib

Musa (peace be upon him) left Egypt in the direction of a city called Madyan, praying for Allah to guide him since he didn't know where he was going, having spent his whole life in Egypt. When he reached Madyan he came to a well surrounded by people drawing water for themselves and their animals. He noticed two women who were standing at the back. Musa asked them what they were doing. They replied that because their father was an old man, his daughters had to come and get water for their flock of sheep. They normally had to wait until all the men had finished taking water before they would get a turn. Musa strode through the crowd and lifted the large bucket full of water from the well on his own. Normally it would have taken several men to lift this bucket. He watered the flock of the sisters and then sat down in the shade of a tree. He prayed that he was in need of whatever good Allah would send him.

When the sisters arrived home, their father, the Prophet Shoaib (peace be upon him), was surprised to see them this early. When they told him what had happened, he asked them to go back and invite Musa home, so they could reward him for his help. Musa (peace be upon him) accepted their invitation and followed them home, where he met with their father and told him his life-story over dinner. Afterwards, one of Shoaib's daughters told him that he should hire Musa because he was strong and trust-worthy. Shoaib asked her how she knew this. She replied that she knew of his strength because he could pull the big bucket full of water out of the well all by himself. She

knew of his trustworthiness because when he was follow-ing her and her sister home, he walked in front of them and asked them to guide him from behind him so they wouldn't feel afraid of being followed by a stranger. Shoaib asked Musa to work for him and said that if he did this for eight years he could marry one of his daughters and become his son-in-law. Shoaib also suggested that an extra two years, making it ten in total would be a kind gesture from Musa. Musa agreed and completed 10 whole years of service.

Receiving Prophethood

After the 10 years were completed, he travelled with his wife back to Egypt, to visit his family there. On the way they lost their way and as night fell, it became very cold. Then, in the distance, on Mount Tur, Musa (peace be upon him) spotted a light. He told his wife to wait there while he went to investigate. If it was a fire he could bring back a burning branch for them to keep warm, and if some-one was there he could ask them for directions. But as Musa approached, he saw a strange sight - a green tree that was on fire, but wasn't burning. And then a most miracu-lous thing happened, Allah spoke to him[v]. Allah told Musa to take off his shoes, as a sign of respect for the blessed land he was standing on, the sacred valley of Tuwa. He told Musa that he was chosen to be a Prophet, to teach people

---

v   This is why Musa is called 'Kaleem'Allah' – the one who spoke with Allah

to worship Allah alone, to pray to Him, and prepare for the Day of Judgement by living a life full of good deeds and giving up sinful habits.

Allah then asked Musa (peace be upon him) what was in his right hand. Musa answered that it was his staff, which he used to lean on, to beat down leaves, and to herd his sheep. Allah asked him to throw it down on the ground, and when he did so it turned into a huge, slithering snake. It was so terrifying that Musa ran away from it. However, Allah called him back, telling him to pick it up without fear. When Musa touched it, the snake turned back into his staff. Then Allah told Musa to put his hand inside his shirt, on his heart. When Musa did this, it removed all fear from his heart, and when he pulled his hand out from his shirt, it was shining brilliantly, like a bright, white lamp. Allah told Musa to go to Pharaoh, to tell him to stop leading his people astray by pretending to be a God, and to stop committing Shirk and worship Allah alone. He should also free the Israelites from their life of slavery.

Musa (peace be upon him) replied to Allah that he was scared Pharaoh would have him executed because of the Egyptian he killed. Allah reassured Musa that Pharaoh would not be able to harm him, because he was being sent by Allah, and Allah would be with him. Musa asked Allah to allow him to take his brother, Haroon (peace be upon him) with him, since he was more eloquent, and they would be able to support and help each other in this most difficult task. Allah accepted this request, and Haroon was also

given Prophethood. Musa returned to his wife and they continued on their way to Egypt. When they got there, Musa was reunited with his family and explained what had happened on the journey and the task that lay ahead for him and his brother.

Return to Egypt

Musa and Haroon (peace be upon them both) went to Pharaoh's palace and told him they had been sent as Prophets by the Lord of the worlds, to bring him a message to free the Israelites, stop pretending to be a God, and worship Allah alone. Pharaoh replied by reminding Musa that he had raised him from when he was a baby and given him everything he could ever want, so that he had lived a life of luxury and ease. But he had betrayed Pharaoh and shown his ungratefulness by first murdering an Egyptian and then bringing this new religion. Musa reminded Pharaoh that the only reason he had ended up in the royal household was because the Egyptians kept the Israelites as slaves and Pharaoh was killing their baby boys. Should he be grateful to the Pharaoh for that? He had killed a man, but that was an accident, it wasn't on purpose, and if he ran, it was because he was afraid of Pharaoh. But since then, Allah had blessed him with Prophethood, and so now it was his duty to spread the truth and demand justice for his people.

In front of his court, Pharaoh sarcastically asked Musa (peace be upon him) who was this Lord of the worlds? Musa replied that He was the Lord of the Heavens and the Earth and all that was between them. Pharaoh turned to those around him and asked, jokingly, if they had heard what Musa had said? Musa knew Pharaoh was trying to

make fun of him, but ignoring this, continued speaking. He told Pharaoh and those around him that Allah was their Lord and the Lord of their ancestors. Pharaoh continued ridiculing Musa, calling him a madman. Musa continued to tell them, that Allah was the Lord of the East and West and everything between them.

Realising that Musa (peace be upon him) didn't care what people thought or said about him, Pharaoh resorted to threatening him with jail. Musa replied by saying he had proof that he was a Prophet of Allah and showed Pharaoh and his advisers the two miracles. However, Pharaoh dismissed these as magic tricks, and challenged Musa to a duel against the best magicians from all over Egypt. Musa accepted the challenge and they agreed for it to take place on the day of the big festival when people from all over Egypt would be gathered in one place.

Duelling the magicians

Finally, the day of the festival came. Pharaoh had gathered the most expert magicians from all over Egypt. They were eager to perform against Musa (peace be upon him) because Pharaoh had promised to make them his special advisers if they were victorious. Musa stood opposite the magicians, with Pharaoh, his advisers and the people of Egypt watching. The magicians asked Musa if he wanted to go first, but he replied that they should go first. They threw down their ropes, sticks and staffs, and it appeared as if they had become a large number of slithering snakes. Seeing this, Musa felt worried that since their magic appeared the same as his miracle, the people watching might get confused and believe that he was a magician as well. However, Allah told him not to fear and to throw down his staff. Allah told him what they had done was magic, and magic was fake, and magicians will never be successful.

So, Musa (peace be upon him) threw down his staff and by the power of Allah it turned into the terrifyingly huge snake. It slithered this way and that, and ate the much smaller magic snakes that were really just ropes, sticks and staffs. The people watching were amazed, but not more so than the magicians. They were experts in their field and knew what was magic and what wasn't. They knew that what they had just seen wasn't magic and so must be a miracle. That meant Musa must be telling the truth and really was a Prophet of Allah. So they fell down in prostration to Allah and said they believed in Allah, the Lord of the worlds, the Lord of Musa and Haroon (peace be upon them both). Pharaoh also couldn't believe what was happening, not only had his best magicians been defeated, but they had also changed their religion, and all in front of everyone watching. This was humiliating for Pharoah.

Secretly, Pharaoh had also realised Musa (peace be upon him) was telling the truth. But because of his arrogance he couldn't admit that he was lying and wasn't really a God, and that Musa, an Israelite who he had raised in his

own home, was a Prophet of Allah. This would mean an end to his kingdom, freeing the Israelites, and an end to the Egyptian way of life. So Pharaoh tried to trick the people by accusing the magicians of working with Musa all along. In fact, he told them, Musa must be their teacher. Pharaoh threatened to cut off their hands and legs and nail them to the trunks of trees as punishment for being traitors and leaving their religion.

However, when the magicians had gone into prostration and believed in Allah, they had been shown the palaces that had been prepared for them in Paradise. So they replied to Pharaoh that he could do whatever he wanted to them. Even if he tortured and killed them, he could only affect the life of this world and if Allah forgave them their sins and blessed them to die as Muslims, they would be granted eternal life in Paradise. It was now impossible for them to go back to their old religion or perform magic, no matter what Pharaoh did to them. As punishment, and in the hope that it would scare people into not following Musa and Haroon (peace be upon them both), Pharaoh crucified the magicians, who died as martyrs.

Punishing the Israelites

Pharaoh's advisers warned him that if he left Musa and Haroon (peace be upon them both) to do as they please, the Egyptians might start converting to their religion and the Israelites might rebel and try to free themselves. So Pharaoh decided he would kill all the Israelite boys. This would act as a warning to any Egyptian who was thinking of following Musa and it would weaken the Israelites, reducing the number of their men. The Israelites complained to Musa that before he was born their sons were being killed and after his coming to them as a Prophet their sons were going to be killed, again. Musa told them to pray to Allah for help and to be patient. He said it might well be Allah's plan to destroy their enemies and make them the owners of the very land in which they were currently slaves.

Pharaoh also spoke to the Egyptian people, asking them who was better, the king who ruled Egypt or this poor Israelite, who could not even speak properly. If Musa (peace be upon him) was telling the truth and really was a Prophet of Allah, why didn't he have bracelets of gold, or Angels protecting him? Pharaoh told them he was going to

kill Musa since otherwise he would lure people away from their religion and cause arguments and fighting between them. If what Musa was saying was true, then let him call on his Lord to protect him. Upon hearing this, one of the people in his court, who secretly believed in Allah, tried to dissuade him. He asked Pharaoh if he was going to kill Musa simply because he believed in Allah, even though he had brought evidence in the form of miracles. He reasoned that if Musa was lying, he would only be harming himself, but if he was telling the truth, then Allah would punish Pharaoh for his behaviour. He reminded him of the people of Nuh and Hud and Saleh and the other Prophets (peace be upon them all), who had been destroyed. If this happened to the Egyptians, who could save them?

But Pharaoh was not interested in listening to reason, and instead thought up of another way to make fun of Musa and Haroon (peace be upon them both). He told his advisors to order the baking of millions of bricks. He wanted them to build the tallest tower ever built, to climb up to the Heavens to see the God of Musa. When the Egyptians would see him do this, he could say with even more authority that Musa's God did not exist, he was imaginary, whereas Pharaoh was in front of them and real, and so more worthy of being worshipped.

Meanwhile, the believer started preaching to the Egyptians, asking them to follow his example and believe in Musa (peace be upon him). He told the Egyptians to do good deeds, to realise the life of this world was short and there would be an afterlife where Allah would judge them and either punish them in Hell or reward them in Paradise. But the Egyptians argued with him, telling him to remain on their religion instead. He replied that while he was calling them to Allah's forgiveness and Paradise, they were calling him to Allah's anger and Hell. He warned them that soon there would come a time when they would remember what he was saying to them, and regret not listening to him. Having said what he could to Pharaoh and the Egyptians, he prayed to Allah for protection. He had put his life at risk revealing his belief in Musa's Prophethood. However, he was willing to take this risk because he loved his people and wanted to see them saved from Allah's punishment.

Allah's punishment

Because Pharaoh and the Egyptians refused to believe Musa and Haroon (peace be upon them both) and continued making fun of and threatening them, Allah started sending punishments upon them. Miraculously, these punishments only affected the Egyptians, not the Israelites. These were warnings to make them realise they were heading towards complete destruction, in this life and the next, but still had time to change course. First came the punishment of drought. The rains stopped falling until the crops and animals started dying, leaving no food or water. Pharaoh blamed this on Musa and his brother bringing bad luck and earning the displeasure of the Egyptian Gods. However, when the Egyptians couldn't bear this anymore, they demanded that Pharaoh should bring back the rains. If he really was a God, why couldn't he do this? Pharaoh knew he had no control over the rains and so was left with no choice but to go to Musa in secret and ask him to pray to Allah to stop His punishment and send rain. He promised Musa that if he did this, he would publicly believe in him and free the Israelites. So Musa prayed to Allah and it began to rain. However, Pharaoh broke his promise and instead announced to the Egyptians that he had brought the rains for his people, as further proof that he was their God.

The next punishment that Allah sent was a flood. It started raining and didn't stop until the Nile burst its banks and the Egyptian farmlands and homes were full of water. Again, this was blamed on Musa but in the end the Egyptians demanded from Pharaoh to stop the rains. Again, Pharaoh had no choice but to secretly beg Musa (peace be upon him) to pray to Allah to end the punishment, again promising that this time he would keep his promise to believe in Musa and free the Israelites. But when Musa prayed to Allah and He stopped the rains, Pharaoh again broke his promise and claimed he was the one who had brought relief to his people.

Further punishments Allah sent upon the Egyptians included a plague of locusts, that ate all the crops and plants; lice, crawling in the hair of every Egyptian, sucking their blood and causing constant itching; frogs,

which croaked and hopped out of every nook and cranny in every house, including every pot and pan; and finally, blood, so that there wasn't a single drop of water to drink but it was mixed with fresh blood, including every well and river. Every time the same pattern repeated itself of blaming Musa (peace be upon him) but then asking him to pray to Allah for relief from the punishment and breaking the promise to believe in him and free the Israelites. During the many years over which these punishments came, one after another, the Israelites continued suffering at the hands of the Egyptians. Allah had told Musa and Haroon (peace be upon them both) to tell their people to make their houses places of worship, since they could not openly declare their belief in Musa or worship Allah.

Parting of the sea

Musa (peace be upon him) was now certain Pharaoh was never going to stop encouraging the Egyptians to commit *Shirk* or free the Israelites. So he prayed to Allah to destroy the riches and wealth He had granted Pharaoh and his advisors and to harden their hearts, so they would not be granted the light of faith until the final punishment of Allah reached them. Allah told Musa He had accepted his prayer, which told Musa that the final punishment of Allah would soon arrive. So Musa and Haroon (peace be upon them both) secretly prepared the Israelites. Not long afterwards, in the middle of the night, Allah told Musa to take the Israelites and escape. When morning came, the Egyptians realised what had happened. When the news reached Pharaoh, he flew into a rage and sent messengers to every part of Egypt to gather his entire army and march after the Israelites.

The Israelites had a head start but soon came to the Red Sea. As they were deciding what to do, the Egyptian army appeared in the distance behind them. They were now trapped, with nowhere to run. As the Egyptian army marched closer, panic started setting in. The Israelites came to Musa and Haroon (peace be upon them both) in desperation, certain they would soon either all be slaughtered by their enemy or pushed into the sea. However, Musa had complete faith in Allah's plan and reassured them that He would show them a way out.

As Pharaoh and his army surrounded the Israelites, Allah told Musa (peace be upon him) to strike the sea with his staff. When he did this, the water began to part, rising up like mountains and leaving a path in the centre. Seeing this incredible miracle, the Israelites faith was strengthened. Musa walked through the Red Sea via this dry path, followed by the Israelites. Pharaoh knew this was a miracle from Allah and so did not plan to enter the sea. However, the Archangel Jibra'il (peace be upon him) came in the form of an Egyptian soldier riding on his horse. He rode in front of Pharaoh, into the sea, his horse neighing to Pharaoh's horse as he passed, causing it to follow him. Pharaoh watched in horror as his horse went forward by itself and

entered the sea, and behind him, the rest of the Egyptian army followed.

As Pharaoh and his army entered the sea, Musa (peace be upon him) and the Israelites exited it on the other side. Allah told Musa to strike the sea again with his staff. When he did this, the mountains of water that were being held in place by the power of Allah were suddenly released and came crashing together. As this was happening, Pharaoh realised the time of his death had arrived. At that moment, desperate to save himself from punishment in the afterlife, he prayed that he believed in no other God but Allah. Jibra'il (peace be upon him) was taking mud from the bottom of the sea and shoving it into Pharaoh's mouth, to stop him from being able to make this prayer. He was worried that given how great Allah's mercy is, He might forgive Pharaoh. However, Allah had already accepted the prayer of Musa, that due to his arrogance and tyranny, Pharaoh would not be able to believe until he saw his death approaching. Believing at that moment and seeking forgiveness is never accepted by Allah. So, Pharaoh and the entire Egyptian army was drowned.

Manna and Salwa

Musa and Haroon (peace be upon them both) now led the Israelites towards *Bait'al-Maqdis* (Jerusalem). This was their homeland, since it was where their ancestor, the Prophet Yaqub had lived before travelling with his family to Egypt to live with his son, the Prophet Yusuf (peace be upon them both). On the way they came across a people worshipping idols. Some of the Israelites asked Musa to make them an idol so they could worship it as well. Musa was incredibly disappointed, reminding them that Allah was the only One worthy of worship and these idols were nothing but statues.

When they reached *Bait'al-Maqdis* they found a people living there who were their enemies and wrong-doers. Musa (peace be upon him) told the Israelites that Allah had specifically chosen this land for them, and so they should make ready to go to war. In the same way Allah had made them victorious over Pharaoh and the Egyptians, He would make them victorious here also. However, the Israelites refused to fight because they were scared of the people. They said they would only enter these lands if the

people who already lived there left on their own. A few brave Israelites, whose faith was strong, tried to encourage the rest to fight, that if they trusted in Allah, Allah would give them victory, but the rest of them refused to listen. They said that if Musa wanted to fight, then he and his Lord could go and fight, they would stay where they were. In desperation, Musa prayed to Allah, that he could not control his people or force them to fight. Allah replied that due to their disobedience and lack of faith, they would be punished by having to wander for 40 years, without having any land to call home.

And so the Israelites became wanderers. However, even during this time Allah's blessings continued descending upon them. He provided nourishment for them in the form of *Manna* and *Salwa*[vi]. When it became too hot, He sent clouds to shade them. When they wanted water, Allah told Musa (peace be upon him) to strike a rock with his staff, causing 12 springs to gush forth, one for each tribe. Despite this, the Israelites complained to Musa that they were tired of eating the same thing every day and asked him to pray to Allah to give them herbs, cucumbers, garlic, lentils, and onions. Musa was disgusted by their ungratefulness and refused to pray to Allah for them, telling them to find such food themselves.

During this time, Allah told Musa (peace be upon him) to fast for 30 days. After completing the 30 days, Musa chewed a plant. Allah asked him why he had done this, to which Musa replied that he wanted to speak to Allah with his breath smelling fresh. Allah told him that there is no smell He likes more than that of a fasting person's breath. So Allah told him to fast for 10 more days. After completing these 40 days, Allah told him to climb up Mount Tur and return to the place he had first spoken with Allah. Musa left Haroon (peace be upon them both) in charge of the Israelites while he was gone.

When Musa (peace be upon him) arrived at the place, Allah again spoke to him. Musa asked Allah that he wanted to see Him, but Allah replied that Musa would not be able to do this. To explain, Allah told Musa to watch

---

vi   There are many different opinions about what these were, one of which is that Manna was a sweet, honey-like sap that the trees produced, and Salwa was a bird, like a quail.

a nearby mountain as He revealed a tiny fraction of His light upon it. When Allah did this, the mountain instantly exploded into pieces of dust, completely vanishing from existence. Seeing this extraordinary sight, Musa fell down unconscious. After a while, when he regained consciousness he sought forgiveness from Allah and announced His glory. Allah gave Musa tablets of stone on which was written the *Taurat* (Torah). He was to take this back to the Israelites as it contained instructions for them on how to live their lives in a way that would please Allah and make their society peaceful and fair. Allah then told Musa that in his absence He had tested the Israelites and a man called Samiri had led them astray.

The golden calf

Musa (peace be upon him) was greatly distressed to hear this and hurried back to his people. There, he found that some of the Israelites had started worshipping a gold statue of a calf. Musa threw down the tablets in anger and grabbed hold of his brother Haroon (peace be upon him) by his beard, asking him why he had let them commit *Shirk*. Haroon told Musa not to blame him. He had tried his best to stop them, but instead of listening to him they had listened to Samiri. He did not take things any further, because he didn't want the Israelites to start fighting each other. Musa turned to Samiri and demanded an explanation. Samiri told Musa that when he left them, he told the people to melt their gold jewellery. Putting it all together, he fashioned a calf and he also mixed in some dirt. This dirt was from the hoofsteps of Jibra'il's horse. On the day the Pharaoh had drowned, Samiri had seen that wherever the Archangel's horse placed its hooves, green grass began to grow. So he had taken some dirt and saved it. This was why the golden calf statue made a 'mooing' sound. Samiri told the Israelites that this was their God and the God of Musa, but Musa had forgotten and gone to the mountain of Tur to try and find him. As a result, many of the Israelites began worshipping it.

As punishment, Musa (peace be upon him) exiled Samiri so he had to leave his people, and cursed him so that he would never want anyone to be near him again, living and dying alone. Turning to his people, Musa asked them if this calf could reply to them, harm them, or benefit them in

any way? If not, how could it be their God, whose miracles they had seen with their own eyes, who had saved them from the tyranny of Pharaoh. Musa then destroyed the calf by grinding it into dust, mixing it with water and giving it to the Israelites to drink. The gold dust stuck to the lips of those who had worshipped the calf, making them stand out. They realised they had committed a most serious sin and asked Allah to forgive them. However, Allah told Musa that for the Israelites to be forgiven, the ones who had committed *Shirk* needed to be killed.

Even when living like slaves under the rule of Pharaoh in Egypt, many Israelites still worshipped Allah, who they knew about from their forefathers, the descendants of the Prophet Yaqub (peace be upon him). However, many Israelites had forsaken their own religion and worshipped the Egyptian Gods and Pharaoh. These were the same people who, upon escaping from Egypt had passed by the people worshipping idols and had asked Musa (peace be upon him) to make them an idol as well. And these same people had worshipped the golden calf. Therefore, Allah's judgement concerning them might have been because He knew that these people would never give up wanting to commit *Shirk* and would lead other Israelites into sin as well.

So it happened that all those whose lips had turned gold upon drinking the water were killed by the others. Then, Musa (peace be upon him) took 70 of the Israelite leaders with him to Mount Tur to seek forgiveness from

Allah. But as they climbed the mountain, Allah punished them for not having stopped their people committing shirk and supporting Haroon in the absence of Musa. A violent earthquake shook the mountain killing all 70 of the Israelite leaders. Musa prayed to Allah for forgiveness for himself and his people, for Allah not to punish all of them for the behaviour of the sinners and criminals amongst them. Allah accepted Musa's prayer and brought them back to life.

Musa (peace be upon him) now returned to his duty of teaching the Israelites the commandments of Allah within the *Taurat* written on the tablets of stone. However, the Israelites would argue with him, and say they are only willing to follow the commands that were easy and would leave the ones they found difficult. Musa explained this is not how faith in Allah and His Revelation works, that it is not up to them to pick and choose what they want to follow. When the Israelites continued arguing and disobeying him, Allah sent Angels to uproot and lift a mountain over their heads like a roof or canopy. They were warned that if they did not change their ways, the mountain would fall upon them, crushing them. Finally, being able to directly see the punishment of Allah, the Israelites listened to what Musa was teaching them.

One day a murder happened amongst the Israelites. In the morning, the dead body of an old man was found. He had been quite wealthy and had many family members who stood to inherit his wealth. But because there were

no witnesses, no-one knew who had killed him. The people came to Musa (peace be upon him) and asked him to pray to Allah for an answer. When he did this, Allah told him to tell the Israelites to slaughter a cow. However, when Musa told them this, they thought he was joking and making it up. Musa reminded them that to lie about what Allah has said is one of the most serious sins and something a Prophet could never do. Instead of finding a cow and slaughtering it, the Israelites asked Musa to ask Allah what kind of cow it should be. So Musa asked Allah and told them it shouldn't be too old or too young. They then asked Musa to ask Allah what colour it should be. So Musa asked Allah and told them it should be a beautiful yellow cow. This still wasn't enough for the Israelites, so they asked Musa to again, ask Allah to give more details about what kind of cow they needed to slaughter. So Musa asked Allah and told them that it should never have been used to do farm work and it should be in perfectly good health.

Now, the Israelites started trying to find such a cow, but this took a long time because none of the cows fulfilled all of the requirements. In fact, they could only find one such cow and the person who owned it refused to sell it to them unless they paid 10 times its weight in gold. Reluctantly, they did so and brought it to Musa (peace be upon him). He ordered them to slaughter the cow and then hit the dead man with a piece of its meat. When they did this a miracle occurred and Allah brought him back to life. Musa asked him who had killed him. He replied it was his nephew and fell back down, dead.

Qarun

Qarun was a relative of Musa (peace be upon him). He was the richest of all the Israelites, having earned his wealth by working for the Pharaoh in Egypt as a spy, telling him what his people were talking about and planning. Even the keys to his treasure were so heavy, it would take many men to lift them. Having all this wealth and power had made Qarun a very arrogant person. He believed it was a sign of Allah being pleased with him, even though he did not care about how he earned his wealth and didn't use it to help others. Because of this, he liked to show off and would go out on long walks wearing his fine clothes and jewellery. Many Israelites would see this and feel jealous,

wishing Allah had given them what He had given Qarun. However, Musa and the wise Israelites would tell them off for thinking like this, instead of understanding that their aim in life should be to please Allah. If they were success-ful in doing this, He would give them Paradise compared to which this whole world was worthless. If they failed to do this, regardless of however wealthy or powerful they were in this life, they would go to Hell and lose everything. They had the example of Pharaoh and the Egyptians fresh in their minds – were they not more wealthy and power-ful even than Qarun? How did that help them against the punishment of Allah? Musa and the wise Israelites would also warn Qarun that Allah did not like arrogance, that instead of showing off he should be grateful for what he had and use it to please Allah to build a home for himself in Paradise.

Qarun wanted to get rid of Musa (peace be upon him) because he didn't want to have to live by the rules of the *Taurat* and do things like give his money to the poor. He wanted to live in a society where the rich and powerful could live like kings and do what they wanted. So he made a plan and paid a woman money to say Musa had committed adultery with her, a major sin. The next time Musa was preaching to the Israelites about sins and their punishments, he also told them the punishment for adultery as written in the *Taurat*. Qarun then asked Musa in front of everyone if the same law applied to him, and Musa said it did. Qarun then called the woman and announced that Musa had committed adultery with this woman. Musa and the rest of the Israelites were shocked to hear this. Musa prayed to Allah and then asked the woman to take an oath and tell the truth. The woman told the truth that she had been given money by Qarun to make up this lie against Musa. Musa thanked Allah for revealing the truth. Allah told Musa that the Earth had been put under his command. Musa cursed Qarun and his wealth to be swallowed by the Earth. In front of many of the Israelites who used to feel jealous of him, Qarun slowly sank into the ground, first up to his ankles, then his knees, then his waist, then his neck, until he completely disappeared. None of his wealth and power could save him from Allah's punishment.

Musa and Khidr

One day Musa (peace be upon him) was giving a speech to the Israelites. One of them asked him which person was the most knowledgeable. As the Prophet of Allah, Musa replied that it was him. But Allah wanted to remind His Prophet that all knowledge comes from Allah, and so He told Musa that at the place the two seas meet, there was someone more knowledgeable than him. Musa asked Allah how he could find this person. Allah told him to take a fish with him on his journey and he would find this person at the place the fish came back to life. So, Musa set out with a servant called Yusha (peace be upon him). They travelled to the coast and walking along it, came to a place two seas came together. They rested there and Musa fell asleep. When he awoke, they carried on travelling. After some time, Musa asked Yusha for some food. Yusha told Musa that he had forgotten to tell him something important. At the place they had rested, while Musa was asleep, he had seen a most extraordinary sight. The fish they had brought with them had come back to life and wriggled into the sea. Musa told him that this was the place they were meant to find the person they were looking for and so they retraced their steps. When they arrived back at that place, they saw a man standing there wrapped in a sheet – this was Khidr (may Allah be pleased with him).

Musa (peace be upon him) asked Khidr (may Allah be pleased with him) to let him travel and spend time with him to learn from him. Khidr told Musa that he had been given knowledge by Allah that Musa didn't have in the same way that Musa had been given knowledge by Allah that he didn't have. Because of this, it would be difficult for Musa to remain patient with him. Musa reassured him that if Allah willed, he would be patient. So Khidr agreed for Musa to travel with him on condition that he did not ask Khidr about why he did the things he did until he told him himself. Musa agreed and so they began their journey. As they walked along the coast they came to a ship. The people recognised Khidr and let them board the ship without having to pay. A bird came and perched on the edge of the boat and dipped its beak into the water. Khidr said to Musa that the example of his knowledge and Musa's

knowledge in comparison to Allah's knowledge was like the amount of water in the bird's beak compared to the sea. Before they got off the boat, Musa was shocked to see Khidr take his axe and make a hole in the boat. Musa asked him why he had done this, especially given the people hadn't even taken any money from them, was he trying to drown them? Khidr replied that he had told Musa he would not be able to be patient. Musa apologised for his forgetfulness.

As they continued travelling, they came across a group of children playing. Khidr (may Allah be pleased with him) walked up to them and killed one of the boys. Musa (peace be upon him) was horrified at this evil act and asked Khidr why he had murdered an innocent child? Khidr again reminded Musa of the condition of their travelling together, and Musa again asked for his forgiveness, asking for just one more chance. Travelling on, they came to a town. Tired and hungry, they asked the townspeople for food and rest. However, they were dealt with very rudely and given nothing. As they were leaving the town, they came across a wall that was falling down. Khidr started repairing it. Musa asked him why he was doing this for free given how they had been treated. Khidr told Musa that he had now used up his last chance and so must leave him. But before that, he would tell Musa why he had done these things.

Khidr (may Allah be pleased with him) said that he damaged the ship because it was owned by poor people who used it to earn a living. But they came from a land where the king was taking every boat that was in good condition, so by damaging it they would not lose it and could repair it afterwards. He told Musa (peace be upon him) he killed the boy because his parents were good, pious people but their son would have grown up to be a bad person and a disbeliever. He would have caused harm to his parents but this way, Allah would replace him with a child who would grow up to be a kind-hearted believer. And finally, Khidr explained that he repaired the wall because it was built on land owned by two orphans. Their father had buried some treasure underneath that wall. If the wall had collapsed, maybe someone else would have found the treasure and taken it. This way they would be able to dig it up when they are older. Khidr told Musa that he had not done any of these things except by the command of Allah. If Musa had been patient, he would have seen many more wondrous things from Khidr.

Yusha

The 40 years of wandering for the Israelites was coming to an end and Musa (peace be upon him) was taking them back towards *Bait'al-Maqdis* (Jerusalem). His brother, Haroon (peace be upon him) had already passed away. Musa had a great desire to enter his people's homeland with them but the Angel of death, Izra'il (peace be upon him) appeared to him before this. Musa slapped him

and knocked out one of his eyes. Izra'il returned back to Allah and told Him that Musa did not want to die. Allah sent him back to Musa with a message to put his hand on the back of an ox. For each hair that came under his hand, he would be granted another year of life. Musa asked the Angel what would happen after those years had passed and was told he would die. So Musa told him that he might as well remove his soul now, and he was grateful he had led his people back to *Bait'al-Maqdis*, even if he did not get to enter it.

After Musa passed away, Yusha was given Prophethood by Allah (peace be upon them both). The Israelites had once again reached *Bait'al-Maqdis* and once again, were told they needed to fight the people who lived there to gain access to their homeland. During the 40 years of wandering, the older Israelites who had been alive during the reign of Pharaoh and were used to being slaves had all passed away. Their children had grown up strong and brave and so unlike their parents, were ready to follow their Prophet Yusha into battle. The battle was long and fierce, but as the Israelites started to get the upper hand, the Sun began to set. Yusha was concerned that if night fell and fighting stopped, their enemy would be able to rest and regroup. So he pointed at the Sun and spoke to it, saying that both of them were fulfilling the command of Allah. He then prayed to Allah to stop the Sun from setting. Allah accepted Yusha's prayer, and the Sun did not set until the Israelites were victorious over their enemies and conquered *Bait'al-Maqdis.*

O Allah, shower peace and blessings upon Your Prophets Musa, Haroon and Yusha, for every letter of every syllable of every word of every language.

The Prophet Dawud

(peace be upon him)

As time passed since the time of Musa, Haroon, and Yusha (peace be upon them all), the Israelites stopped following their teachings and started behaving like tyrants against other people, who were not as powerful as they were. They forgot how it used to be when they were being persecuted by people more powerful than them and they were the weak, powerless ones. So Allah punished them by sending mighty and terrible enemies against them who enslaved and killed them, drove them out of *Bait'al-Maqdis*, separating their families and scattering them.

Several generations later, Allah sent them a Prophet called Shammil (peace be upon him). The Israelites asked Shammil to appoint a king who could lead them in battle.

Shammil asked them to think very carefully about what they were asking for. They had a history of saying one thing and then doing another, of acting courageous but when the time came to fight, of refusing. The Israelites reassured him that they desperately wanted to go back to their homeland and be reunited with their families, and so they were ready to fight. So, Shammil chose a young man called Talut (may Allah be pleased with him) to be their king. However, the Israelites complained that they didn't think he had made the right decision. Talut wasn't from one of their respected tribes or wealthy. Shammil explained that Allah had chosen him and blessed him with knowledge and strength. Furthermore, as a sign of his kingship, Allah would bless the Israelites by returning the Ark to them, carried by Angels, which would bring them peace. This was a chest containing relics left by the family of Musa and Haroon (peace be upon them both - such as their staffs and the original *Taurat* tablets), which had been taken from the Israelites by their enemies.

Talut (may Allah be pleased with him) led an army of Israelites back to *Bait'al-Maqdis*. On the way they came to the river Jordan. Everyone was thirsty and wanted to drink, but Allah inspired Talut to test his people by telling them not to drink any more than a handful of water from the river. He told them that only those who passed this test would be allowed to go on with him. Most of the Israelites failed, disobeying their king and drinking their fill from the river. Only roughly 300 Israelites followed his orders and

so went on with him to *Bait'al-Maqdis.* There, they saw the huge army of their enemy, led by Jalut, a powerful warrior who looked like a giant. Talut and his companions were afraid but had faith and prayed to Allah for help in overcoming the disbelievers. They knew that if Allah willed a small army could defeat a bigger army.

Jalut challenged them to send a warrior forward to fight him in a duel. Talut (may Allah be pleased with him) looked for a volunteer from his army but everyone was too scared, thinking they would not stand a chance. Then, a boy called Dawud (peace be upon him) stepped forward with his slingshot and said he would fight Jalut. Everyone knew that he was a pious young man who only feared Allah. At first Talut refused, looking for someone else to volunteer. But when no-one else did, and Dawud put himself forward again, Talut agreed, thinking this must be Allah's plan. As Dawud strode forward, Jalut laughed at the puny little soldier sent to fight him. However, before he even had a chance to draw his sword, Dawud loaded a stone in his slingshot, prayed to Allah, and fired. The stone hit Jalut between the eyes like a bullet from a gun, instantly killing him. His soldiers watched in horror as their mighty commander was killed by the weakest soldier of the Israelite army. They turned and fled in terror.

Dawud (peace be upon him) grew up to also be a Prophet of Allah and he became king of the Israelites. He was very pious, every night he would wake up and worship Allah and every other day he would fast. He would remem-

ber Allah and cry, so often that the tears had formed ridges on his cheeks. He was given Revelation for his people called the *Zabur*. One of the miracles Allah granted him was an exceptionally beautiful voice. When he would recite from the *Zabur*, the birds, animals and even mountains would join in glorifying Allah. People listening would stop what they were doing, lost in the beauty of his voice reciting the beautiful words of Allah.

Allah also blessed him with wisdom so he would make fair judgement between his people. And despite being king, he would go out amongst his people in disguise, so he could hear their honest opinion of him. If he heard them praising him, this only increased him in humbleness. Another miracle he was granted was that he could melt iron with his bare hands, allowing him to work as a blacksmith without needing a furnace and tools. He used to make suits of chainmail for the Israelites to help them in battle, and would buy food for himself and his family from the money he earned doing this, rather than using money from the treasury.

O Allah, shower peace and blessings upon Your Prophets Shammil and Dawud, for every moment of thirst and every pang of hunger of every fasting slave, and as much as You love the fragrance of their breath.

The Prophet Sulayman
(peace be upon him)

The Prophet Dawud had a son called Sulayman, who was also blessed by Allah to be a Prophet (peace be upon them both). Like his father, Sulayman was also blessed with great wisdom. In fact, even as a child he would sometimes give his opinion on cases that were brought in front of his father, and Dawud would choose the ruling of his son over his own. For example, one day two women came to Dawud's court with a baby, each claiming that the child was theirs. They said they were walking together with their children when a wolf attacked, killed and dragged away one child. Each claimed the wolf had killed the other

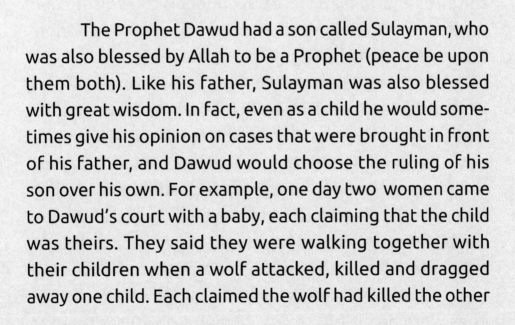

woman's child and the child who was left was theirs. When Dawud had heard both women's stories, he decided the child belonged to the older woman. However, before they left the court, Sulayman said that he would have the child cut in half so both women could share equally. Upon hearing this the younger woman was horrified and begged him not to do this, that she would prefer the other woman to have him. Since the real mother would never be able to accept her child being killed in this way, this told Sulayman that the younger woman was in fact the real mother and his father's judgement was changed.

Allah blessed Sulayman (peace be upon him) with being not only a Prophet but also a king, like his father before him. However, not only did he rule over people, but the birds and animals were put under his control; he could understand their speech and communicate with them. This meant he had a huge army unlike the world had ever seen. One day, when he was marching through a valley, he heard an ant speaking to its fellow ants, warning them that Sulayman was coming with his soldiers and if they did not enter their homes, they would be crushed. Sulayman smiled upon hearing the ant's speech and thanked Allah. He prayed to Allah to allow him to be truly grateful for all the blessings Allah had bestowed upon him and his parents before him, and to make him a righteous slave.

One of Sulayman's favourite things were his horses. They were beautiful, strong, graceful creatures that carried his armies into battle. He would spend his spare time

with them, stroking and admiring them. One day he was so absorbed in doing this that much of the day passed. He didn't notice until the Sun began to set. Sulayman (peace be upon him) realised his love for his horses was distracting him from the worship of Allah, and so he gave them away and asked for Allah to forgive him. He prayed for Allah to give him a kingdom that would not be given to anyone after him. Allah accepted his prayer and rewarded His Prophet for giving up the thing he loved for His sake by giving Sulayman control of the wind and command over the Jinn. When he wanted to travel from one place to another he would sit on a rug and the wind would carry it wherever he commanded. This would allow him to cross, in a morning or evening, the distance it would normally take a month to travel. And just as he had an army of human soldiers, he had an army of Jinn. Other Jinn would work as builders for him, constructing huge buildings, or divers bringing pearls up from the bottom of the oceans. Those who disobeyed him were chained and jailed.

Kingdom of Saba

One day Sulayman (peace be upon him) noticed one of the birds of his court, the *Hud-Hud*, was not present. He asked about where he was, threatening to punish him if he did not have a good excuse. However, before long the *Hud-Hud* returned and told Sulayman that he had discovered a rich kingdom in the land of Saba where a queen called

Bilqis ruled over a people who worshipped the Sun. Sulayman wrote a letter and told *Hud-Hud* to take it to Bilqis and to return with her reply. When Bilqis received the letter, she called her advisors and discussed it with them. She told them she had received a letter from Sulayman who was calling them to not be arrogant, give up worshipping the Sun and believe in Allah. Her advisors told her that they had a large kingdom with a powerful army, so if Sulayman attacked them, they could defend themselves. However, Bilqis wanted to try and avoid going to war. So she replied by sending very expensive gifts to Sulayman, to develop a friendship, an alliance.

When the gifts from the kingdom of Saba reached Sulayman (peace be upon him) he rejected them and sent them back. He sent a message telling them he did not need their wealth. Allah had given him more than what He had given them, and he was not interested in worldly things. This was their last chance to give up their *Shirk* and worship Allah otherwise he would send an army they could not resist. Upon receiving this reply, Bilqis decided to go to Sulayman to meet him in person. When the *Hud-Hud* brought this news back to Sulayman, he asked his court if anyone could bring him her throne before she arrived. The most powerful Jinn stood up and said he could bring it before Sulayman rose from his seat. However, a man called Asif ibn Barkhiya said he could bring the throne within the blink of an eye. Asif was one of Sulayman's companions who was very pious and had been blessed to know the *Ism-*

e-Azam, the greatest name of Allah, with which if a prayer is made, it is sure to be accepted. When Sulayman saw Bilqis' throne instantly appear in front of him upon acceptance of Asif's prayer, he gave thanks to Allah. He told his workers to disguise the throne so it wasn't instantly recognisable. In preparation for Bilqis' arrival, Sulayman also had a new floor built in the palace made of glass, underneath which was a pool of water.

When Bilqis arrived she saw the huge throne and became puzzled. It looked like her throne, but not quite. Anyway, that would be impossible given her throne was in her palace nearly 2000 miles away. Then, when she entered the palace, she raised her dress to stop it getting wet. However, when she stepped on the floor her feet remained dry but it was as if she was walking on water. She realised the floor was made of glass. Bilqis considered everything

she knew about Sulayman (peace be upon him). He began his letters by mentioning Allah. He constantly prayed and thanked Allah and did not display any arrogance despite being the most powerful king alive. He was not interested in worldly treasures and had rejected her gifts, and he was only concerned with stopping her people committing *Shirk*. His companions could carry out miraculous acts such as transporting her throne. She considered whether he was truly the Prophet of Allah and whether her people had been living under an illusion in worshipping the Sun in the same way this glass floor had made her believe the illusion she was walking on water. Faith had entered her heart and she accepted Islam and prayed for forgiveness from Allah. Sulayman married Bilqis, and then she returned to her people, who also accepted Islam.

Sulayman (peace be upon him) finished rebuilding *Masjid'al-Aqsa* in *Bait'al-Maqdis*, a project that his father, the Prophet Dawud (peace be upon them both) had started in his lifetime. He used the Jinn to do this. Upon its completion, Sulayman prayed for Allah to forgive all the sins of any person who leaves their home with the intention of praying in this Mosque. The Prophet Muhammad (peace be upon him) also prayed for Allah to accept this prayer. Sulayman would keep the Jinn busy doing work. They did not enjoy this; before Sulayman no-one else had been able to rule over them in this way and they considered this a form of slavery and punishment, but were scared of disobeying him. When Sulayman's soul departed from this

world he was sitting on his throne, leaning on his staff. Because of this, he stayed upright, and the Jinn kept working, thinking their king still alive. It was only when a wood-worm gnawed through the stick, weakening it enough to snap under his weight, causing Sulayman's body to fall to the floor, did the Jinn realise their master was dead and then quickly escaped.

O Allah, shower peace and blessings upon Your Prophet Sulayman, for every step of the feet of the animals of the Earth and every beating of the wings of the birds of the sky.

The Prophet Uzair
(peace be upon him)

Again, a time came upon the Israelites that they started moving away from the teachings of their Prophets and behaving as tyrants against other people. So again, Allah sent against them powerful enemies who invaded their lands, including *Bait'al-Maqdis*, destroyed *Masjid'al-Aqsa*, burning the *Taurat*, killing, enslaving and scattering the Israelites. During this time, Allah sent them a Prophet called Uzair (peace be upon him). One day Uzair was passing through some ruins, where he got off his donkey and sat down in the shade. He had some food and drink with him which he had prepared for himself. As he looked around, he wondered to himself how Allah would bring such ruins back to life. This was not because he did not believe Allah could do it, but he was curious as to how it would happen. Allah planned to answer the question of His Prophet, so He sent the Angel of death to take his life.

Uzair (peace be upon him) remained dead for 100 years before Allah sent an Angel to bring him back to life. The Angel then asked Uzair how long he had been asleep, to which he replied a day, or part of a day. Uzair thought that he must have fallen asleep while resting in the ruins, tired from his journey. The Angel told him that in fact, he had been dead for 100 years. He told him to look at his food and drink, which were still fresh, but then to look at his donkey, which was just a pile of bones. In front of his eyes, through the power of Allah, the bones of the donkey came together and became covered in flesh, until the donkey was brought back to life and standing in front of him. Uzair praised Allah, the All Powerful, his question had been answered.

Uzair (peace be upon him) then rode his donkey back to his neighbourhood and house. There he found a very old woman who was blind and disabled. Uzair asked her if this was the house of Uzair. The old lady started crying, saying that this was the house of Uzair but it had been so many years since she had heard anyone mention that name, the people had forgotten him. Uzair told her who he was and how Allah had taken his life 100 years ago but now brought him back to life. The old lady said that Uzair was someone who prayed for the sick and his prayers were always answered. So to prove he was who he said he was,

she asked him to pray for her to be cured. Uzair prayed to Allah and then passed his hand over her eyes, causing her to be able to see again. He then held her hand and asked her to stand by the power of Allah, which she did. When she looked at him, she confirmed that he was indeed Uzair. A hundred years ago she used to be his maidservant, and recognised him since he looked exactly as he had done before he disappeared.

The old maidservant now went to the neighbourhood where Uzair's children and grandchildren lived and told them the good news. They did not believe her at first, but she told them how he had cured her the way he used to cure the sick by praying to Allah. They came to him (peace be upon him), and his son said that his father had a mole between his shoulders. When they lifted Uzair's shirt, they found the same mole between his shoulders. The good news spread quickly among the Israelites and they flocked to him. They told him how they no longer had any copies of the *Taurat* and no-one among them who knew it. Uzair used to be known as someone who knew the entire *Taurat* by heart, and so they asked him to write it down for them. So Uzair sat under the shade of a tree, surrounded by his family and the Israelites. Allah sent an Angel with a light that he put into Uzair's chest, and he recited the *Taurat* for them, word for word exactly as it had been revealed to Musa (peace be upon them both).

O Allah, shower peace and blessings upon Your Prophet Uzair, for every second of every minute of every hour of every day of every week of every month of every year.

The Prophets Zakariyya and Yahya

(peace be upon them both)

Some centuries before the birth of the Prophet Muhammad (peace be upon him), lived a pious man called Imran (may Allah be pleased with him), who was the Imam of *Masjid'al-Aqsa*, and Zakariyya (peace be upon him), a Prophet of Allah. They were married to two sisters. The wife of Imran was called Hannah (may Allah be pleased with her). Hannah used to pray to Allah that if He blessed her with a son, she would give him up for Allah, to follow in the footsteps of his father. Allah accepted her prayer and

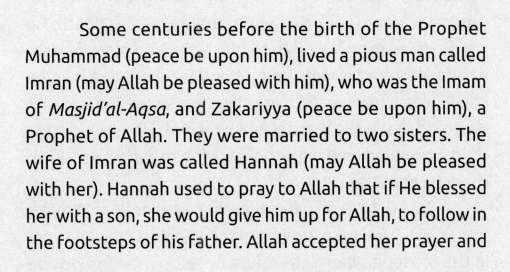

she became pregnant. However, when she gave birth, she was surprised to deliver a baby girl. She had expected the baby to have been a boy, since during those times it was only boys who were given up to serve the Mosque and the religion. However, she knew that Allah knows best, and it was her job to be grateful for His blessings rather than to question Him. Hannah named her daughter Maryam (may Allah be pleased with her) and prayed to Allah to protect her and any children she would go on to have, from Shaitan. As Maryam grew up, Hannah kept her promise to Allah and put her in service of *Masjid'al-Aqsa*. By this time her father, Imran had passed away. So it ended up being her step-uncle, Zakariyya who took care of Maryam.

Zakariyya (peace be upon him) didn't have any children of his own. As the Prophet of the Israelites he was very troubled by what he saw of his people. They needed constant guidance. He had become an old man and worried what would happen to his people after his death. He would often pray for Allah to bless him and his wife with a child, despite his weakening bones and greying hair, he knew Allah had never left his prayers unanswered and that He could make the impossible possible. He prayed for a child who could lead his people after him, who could keep them on the straight path.

Zakariyya (peace be upon him) arranged for Maryam (may Allah be pleased with her) to stay in a special room in the Mosque where she could have privacy and not be disturbed while worshipping Allah. When it was her turn,

she would clean the Mosque and perform the other duties required of her. She grew up to be a very pious young woman, so much so that the Angels would say to her that Allah had chosen and purified her over all other women, and the Prophet Muhammad (peace be upon him) told us that Maryam was one of four perfect women in the history of humanity. Whenever Zakariyya would visit her, he would find out-of-season fruit in her room. When he asked her where this had come from, she replied it was from Allah and He could give whatever He wanted to whomever He pleased. In that very instant, Zakariyya prayed to Allah with complete faith and humility, that if He could give Mariam out-of-season fruits, then similarly, He could give Zakariyya and his wife a child even though they were now far too old to have children.

Yahya

Allah accepted his Prophet's prayer and sent Angels to bring him the good news of a son called Yahya (peace be upon him), a name the world had not heard before. Zakariyya (peace be upon him) was overjoyed and asked Allah for a sign to know when his wife had become pregnant. Allah told him that his sign would be that for three days he would not be able to speak. Allah blessed Yahya on the day he was born. Even as a child, he would avoid playing with other children, preferring to spend his time remembering Allah. He grew up to be pious and wise, and very kind and

gentle, especially to his parents. To his father's delight, he was also granted Prophethood by Allah.

As was often the case with Prophets sent to the Israelites, a group of them eventually turned against Zakariyya (peace be upon him) and their hatred towards him grew until they decided to kill him. The time came when, despite being an old man, he had to flee from them. Coming across a hollow tree, he hid inside, but Shaitan led them to his hiding place. The people brought a saw and starting cutting the tree down. When the saw reached Zakariyya's skin, Allah told him that if he screamed in pain, He would turn the Earth upside down and rain down punishment upon the Israelites. So Zakariyya stayed silent as they sawed through him, using his dying moments to be a mercy to his people.

After his father was martyred, Yahya (peace be upon him) continued his mission. He preached to the Israelites to worship Allah alone and remember Him often, to regularly perform prayer and fast, and to give in charity from their wealth. However, what he liked doing most was spending his time remembering Allah while roaming the wilderness with the animals and trees, eating leaves and locusts and drinking spring water. Even the king at the time respected Yahya's opinion. He had fallen in love with his niece, but Yahya told him he couldn't marry her according to the law of the *Taurat*. This had made her very angry, since she wanted to be queen, and so one night she visited the king and got him drunk and started dancing in front of him. The king thought she looked even more beautiful than usual and desperately wanted her, but she refused unless he gave her a gift. The king replied that he would give her whatever she asked for, so she asked for Yahya's head. Caught up in his desire for her, the king gave the order to his soldiers who executed Yahya (peace be upon him) and brought the head to the palace. Allah says He also blessed Yahya on the day he died, and on the day he will be resurrected on the Day of Judgement.

O Allah, shower peace and blessings upon Your Prophets Zakariyya and Yahya, for every raised hand, for every bowed head, for every prostration, for every tear shed, for every trembling heart of every supplicating slave.

The Prophet Isa
(peace be upon him)

One day, while Maryam (may Allah be pleased with her) was walking alone outside of *Masjid'al-Aqsa*, a man appeared before her. Maryam became scared in case he was going to attack her and prayed to Allah for protection. However, the man told her not to be afraid and revealed that he was the Archangel Jibra'il (peace be upon him). He had come to Maryam to give her the good news of a baby that would be born to her. Maryam asked in surprise how she could have a baby when she had never even touched a man, let alone have a husband. Jibra'il reminded her that Allah can do as He pleases and there is no limit to His power. The Archangel blew upon her and miraculously, she became pregnant.

Maryam (may Allah be pleased with her) knew that as the pregnancy progressed and its signs started to show, people would start gossiping and wondering who the father is, accusing her of committing a most serious sin since she was not married. So before that time she left *Masjid'al-Aqsa* and travelled to the city of Bethlehem. As the pregnancy neared its end and the pains of childbirth began, Maryam was standing near a palm tree, holding onto its trunk for support. She was not only in physical pain but also extremely anxious how she would explain to people that her child was a miracle from Allah and had no father. She wished she had died before all this and people had forgotten about her.

Just then, she heard a voice telling her not to worry. It told her that if she needed to drink, Allah had caused a spring to gush nearby, and if she shook the trunk of the palm tree, fresh dates would drop that she could eat. The voice also reassured her, that if anyone questioned her, to tell them she was fasting for the sake of Allah and so couldn't reply. The fasts of the Israelites included not being allowed to talk. Maryam (may Allah be pleased with her) gave birth to a baby boy and called him Isa (peace be upon him). Jibra'il (peace be upon him) had previously told her that Allah had chosen for her to have a son who would become a great Prophet, honoured in this world and the hereafter, that this would be his name and he would speak to people whilst still a baby.

When Maryam (may Allah be pleased with her) returned to her people, exactly what she expected happened. They started questioning her, telling her she had brought shame on her pious family. In response, Maryam pointed to her son. They started ridiculing her, asking her how she expected them to talk to a baby. Had she gone mad, or did she think them fools? But to everyone's surprise, Isa (peace be upon him) spoke, telling the people he was sent by Allah to be their Prophet, to be kind and dutiful to his mother, and to worship Allah and give in charity. Isa prayed to Allah for peace the day he was born, the day he will die, and the day he will be raised again. And so already, Isa had brought two miracles to prove his Prophethood to the Israelites; he was born without a father, and he spoke to his people whilst still a baby.

As he grew up, he found the Israelites to have left the way of their Prophets (peace be upon them all). Their religious leaders, the Rabbis, were focussed on the rules, and used these to keep their people under control. It was almost as if following the rules had become more important than worshipping and trying to please Allah, or behaving in a kind way to other people, especially the poor and needy. For many of the Israelites, love of this world and accumulating wealth had become their religion. So, Allah now sent a new Revelation, the *Injil*, and through this, Isa (peace be upon him) tried to bring the Israelites back onto the straight path. The leaders of the Israelites, their Rabbis, and the rich and powerful among them were threatened

by this new Prophet and his message, and so rejected him, claiming he was a liar and not really a Prophet.

This was despite the many miracles Allah blessed him with, which proved what he was saying was true. He could tell people what they had eaten, even if it was in complete secret, and what they had stored in their houses. He could heal the blind and the leper, by passing his hands over their eyes and their bodies. He could create the shape of a bird out of clay and when he blew into it, by the power of Allah, it would come to life and fly away. On a few occasions, he even prayed to Allah and brought people who had died back to life. But those who were arrogant and stubborn dismissed these as magic tricks. However, the number of people following him was increasing and this was making the Rabbis and leaders of the Israelites worried that they would lose power over their own people.

The people closest to Isa (peace be upon him) were his disciples. On one occasion, Isa told his disciples to fast for 30 days. When they had completed this, his disciples asked him to pray to Allah for a miracle. They wanted a table to descend from the Heavens, covered with food and drink for them to enjoy. Isa warned them not to ask him for such miracles, out of fear of Allah. This was because miracles are usually sent to convince disbelievers and are often followed by the punishment of Allah. However, the disciples said they were only asking for this as a celebration and so they could see the power of Allah with their own eyes which would increase the certainty of their faith.

Isa gave in to their request and prayed to Allah to fulfil their wishes. Allah accepted the prayer of His Prophet, but warned that if after seeing this miracle any of them disbelieved, He would punish them with a punishment He had not previously sent upon the people of this world. This became a festival day and all Israelites, rich and poor, were invited to eat from the Heavenly table. And despite thousands eating from it, the food and drink did not finish, and all who ate were cured from any illnesses they had.

Sometimes Isa (peace be upon him) would walk on water. His disciples were astounded by this and asked him how he did it. Isa told them it was because he had complete faith in Allah. They said they also had complete faith and so he told them to come with him. However, when they walked with him on the water and saw some waves on the surface of the sea, they started drowning. Isa asked them what had happened, to which they replied that seeing the waves had frightened them. Isa told them that if they had been more afraid of the Lord of the waves, they would not have sunk. Another time Isa took some dirt from the ground into his hands and opening one hand, revealed stones, and opening the other, revealed gold. He asked his disciples which they preferred. The disciples replied they liked the gold, but Isa told them that to him, they were both the same.

The Rabbis and leaders of the Israelites came up with a new plan to get rid of Isa (peace be upon him). At this time in history, the Romans ruled over Palestine. So,

they went to the Roman governor of *Bait'al-Maqdis* and told him the reason Isa was gathering a following of Israelites was because he was planning to rebel and overthrow the governor. This led to the Roman governor sending his soldiers to capture and kill Isa. In some stories it says Isa was given knowledge of this plan by Allah, and so he asked his disciples who would be willing to have his image changed to look like his Prophet in exchange for Paradise? One of them volunteered, after which Allah raised Isa into the Heavens. When the Roman soldiers arrived, they captured and eventually crucified the disciple. In other stories it says one of Isa's followers, who had betrayed him and led the Roman soldiers to him, had his appearance changed to look like Isa, and was the one who ended up being crucified. Either way, the Rabbis and Israelite leaders were satisfied because they believed they had gotten rid of Isa. However, his disciples knew the truth.

The Prophet Muhammad told us that when the Day of Judgement is near, Allah will send Isa again (peace be upon them both). He will follow the Qur'an and the example of the Prophet Muhammad as a Muslim, and he will lead us in battle against the *Dajjal* before finally killing him. After this will be a period of peace, during which he will get married and have children. When he dies, he will be buried alongside the Prophet Muhammad and his two friends, Abu-Bakr and Umar (may Allah be pleased with them both), in the Mosque of the Prophet in Madina.

O Allah, shower peace and blessings upon Your Prophet Isa, for every patient, for every physician, for every disease, for every cure.

Why are there so many religions in the world today?

Islam – the religion of all the Prophets

Allah has a system of doing things. He sends Prophets to communities, sometimes with a Revelation, to tell them about Himself, how to worship Him, and how to live their lives in a peaceful and fair way in a community. The Prophet Muhammad told us Allah sent a total of 124,000 Prophets, starting with the Prophet Adam and ending with him (peace be upon them all). All of these Prophets taught the religion of Islam (which can be translated as peace through submission to Allah). However as human society developed, the teachings of each Prophet and the Revelations they were sent with were all slightly different while having the same basic message – to follow the Prophet, only worship the one true God, Allah in the way that He instructed us to, to do good deeds and stop ourselves from committing sins, to develop good character and help the creation of Allah. For this reason, in reality, they were all Muslims, preaching the version of Islam Allah sent them with.

Corruption of Divine Revelations and Prophetic teachings

In the Qur'an, Allah tells us the stories of some of the Prophets and how only a few people from their communities believed in the message they were sent with. After the Prophets passed away and over time as generations passed, the Revelations that they came with and their teachings were changed. This was by powerful people, like kings or religious leaders, who didn't want to have to follow the rules like everyone else.

The Prophet Musa (peace be upon him) came to the Jews with the *Taurat* (Torah). After he passed away, Allah tells us how over time, some Jewish leaders stopped following his teachings and changed the *Taurat*. When Allah sent the Prophet Isa (peace be upon him), he was sent to the Jews with a new revelation, the *Injil* (Gospel). But most of the Jews did not believe in him as a Prophet. The ones who did became Christians. He was eventually taken up by Allah into the Heavens and again, over time some Christian leaders changed the *Injil*. They taught that the Prophet Isa (peace be upon him) had been killed (crucified on the cross), resurrected back to life three days later, and that he was actually God, or the son of God. They also taught that even though Isa and the *Injil* said they should follow all

the laws Musa came with in the *Taurat*, Allah had now told them they did not need to follow any of these rules or laws.

Similarly, when the Prophet Muhammad (peace be upon him) was sent by Allah as the final Prophet with the Qur'an, most of the Jews and Christians refused to believe in him as a Prophet, even though the original *Taurat* and *Injil* had contained descriptions of the final Prophet and how to recognise him.

Jews, Christians and Muslims

This explains why we have Judaism, Christianity and Islam, even though as Muslims we believe that Musa and Isa (peace be upon them both) were both Muslims, preaching the version of Islam Allah sent them with. When the *Injil* was revealed to Isa, all the Jews should have followed him and become Christians. Similarly, when the Qur'an was revealed to the Prophet Muhammad all the Christians should have followed him and become Muslims. Since the religion, the version of Islam that Allah sent His Prophets with, changed over time, in the world today there are major differences between the three Abrahamic faiths (Islam, Christianity and Judaism). This is further compounded by the changes the Jews and Christians made to their religions over the centuries. So, even though we believe the original *Taurat* and *Injil* are true Revelations from Allah,

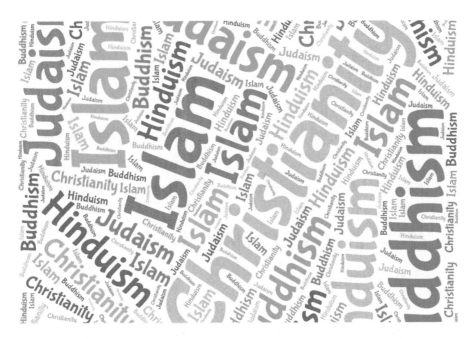

their original versions are no longer available and even if they were, they have been replaced by the Qur'an.

In the context of this book, this especially applies to stories found in the current version of the *Taurat* regarding the Prophets (and therefore the *Injil*, in which the *Taurat* makes up the Old Testament). In all of these stories the Prophets of Allah are portrayed in a negative light, and even described as having committed some of the worst sins. As Muslims we believe that Allah sent the Prophets as examples for their communities, showing them how to live their life according to Allah's Revelation and in a way that would please Him. We believe Allah kept the Prophets free from sin for this reason. Therefore, we do not believe these stories, we reject them absolutely and do not repeat them.

Regarding the Qur'an, as Muslims we do not believe it has or can be changed since Allah has taken it upon Himself to prevent this from happening. He tells us about this in the Qur'an itself. As proof of this, the copies of the *Mus'haf* (written Qur'an) we have today and the oldest versions discovered from close to the time the Prophet was alive (nearly 1400 years ago), are exactly the same.

Other major world religions

This explains why we have the three Abrahamic faiths but what about other major world religions like Hinduism, Buddhism, and Sikhism? Hinduism and Buddhism are ancient religions, thousands of years old. If we look at their teachings, many of them are similar to those found in the Abrahamic faiths so it is probable that these religions started as an ancient version of Islam, by a Prophet or Prophets sent with Revelation that we have not been told about in the Qur'an. Indeed, we can find descriptions matching the Prophet Muhammad (peace be upon him) and his companions (may Allah be pleased with them all) in the Hindu holy books.

Buddhists don't believe in a God but do believe in an Ultimate Reality, which we can reach through meditation and giving up the things of this world. This is exactly how the Prophets, their companions and the *Awliyah-Allah*

(friends of Allah, or saints) used to live their lives. Like with Judaism and Christianity, over time there would have been changes made to these religions, and most of their followers would not have followed later Prophets that Allah sent with new Revelations. This would explain why we still have these ancient religions but no longer upon the right path (*Sirat'al-Mustaqim*).

Sikhism is a newer religion, started about 500 years ago by Guru Nanak, who was followed by nine other Gurus, and their holy book is called the Guru Granth Sahib. Since Guru Nanak was born after the Prophet Muhammad (peace be upon him), it is impossible for him to be a Prophet. This also means the Guru Granth Sahib cannot be Revelation from Allah. However, if we look at the teachings of Sikhism they are similar to what Islam teaches us. In fact, many of the Gurus including Guru Nanak had very close Muslim friends who were of the *Awliyah-Allah*. One of these was Baba Farid (may Allah have mercy upon him), and some of his writings have been included in the Guru Granth Sahib. However, as Muslims we believe that a revelation from Allah cannot be changed except by Allah Himself, which He does by sending another Prophet. The Prophet Muhammad (peace be upon him) was the final Prophet sent with the final Revelation, the Qur'an. Allah tells us He has perfected our religion for us, which tells us it is meant to be followed until the Day of Judgement. Therefore, no further changes are required, so there is no need for future Prophets or

Revelations. So Muslims would only agree with the parts of Sikhism which match with the teachings of Islam.

Interfaith dialogue

As Muslims, talking with people of other faiths to learn more about their beliefs and practices, and educating them about Islam is a praiseworthy act. But we should try not to argue about how their religion is wrong and ours is right. This will drive most people further away from Islam, not towards it. If we want to teach people about Islam the best way to do this is by learning about it ourselves and living our life in the beautiful way of our Prophet (peace be upon him). When people see our good character and realise this is what Islam teaches, they will want to find out more about it and if Allah blesses them, may even become Muslims themselves.

We should also never judge someone and say that they are going to Hell because they are not a Muslim. This is not our job, only Allah knows if someone is going to Paradise or Hell. Some of the biggest enemies of the Prophet (peace be upon him) ended up converting to Islam and becoming his companions (e.g. Abu Sufyan, may Allah be pleased with him). There are people who have spent their whole lives as followers of another religion, or atheists,

who convert to Islam in their old age, and by doing so, all their bad deeds are forgiven, and they die with less sins than people who lived their whole life as Muslims. In fact, the Prophet (peace be upon him) told us that we have no guarantee that even if we live our whole life as Muslims, that we will die as a Muslim, and so this should be something we pray for every day.

Conclusion

In conclusion, as Muslims we believe in the final Prophet of Allah, Muhammad (peace be upon him) and the final Revelation, the Qur'an, which Allah has promised to protect from being changed or corrupted. There are many other religions in the world, many of which are older versions of Islam given to previous Prophets, whose teachings and Revelations have been changed over time. However, not all religions are previous versions of Islam. There are religions that were started by people who were not Prophets, under the influence of Shaitan and their own *Nafs*.

O Allah, shower peace and blessings upon all Your Prophets, from Adam to Muhammad, the ones You have revealed and the ones You have kept hidden, upon their families, companions, descendants and true followers, and all of Your Angels, as much as the ink of Your words, to the extent of Your knowledge, by the power of Your will, and for every moment of time.

Jahannam[vii]

The first time the people destined for *Jahannam* (Hell) will see it, will be on the Day of Judgement. It will still be 100 years distance from them when it will see them, and they will see it. It will be walking towards them on four legs, each tied with 70,000 chains, each chain held by 70,000 Angels. When Hell sees them, it will become enraged. They will hear the dreadful sound of it breathing, it will shake with fury and scream with rage, almost bursting.

If we were to drop a stone from the top of Hell, it would take 70 years to reach the bottom. Hell has seven gates and seven levels. Its fire has burned so hot and for so long that it is now a black fire. Within Hell itself there

vii   The descriptions in this section are from the Qur'an and Hadith literature regarding what will happen to a non-Muslim after death. These are purposefully graphic (they are meant to serve as the most severe warning against not accepting the message of the Prophets - peace be upon them all) and may be scary for little children.

are many different types of punishment. There is *Zaqqum*, a thorny plant they will have to eat but will stick in their throats. They will always be thirsty but all they will have to drink is boiling water and *Ghisleen*, which is a mixture of pus and blood. There is a mountain called *Sa'ud*, and people will be thrown from the top of this. There is an area called *Zamharir* which is as cold and freezing as the rest of Hell is hot and boiling. There will be many strange biting and stinging creatures (imagine huge, terrifying insects and reptiles). Metal chains will be put through their bodies, and they will have burning clothes.

The people suffering these punishments will try to blame Shaitan, and demand for him to help them. He will tell them that Allah made them a promise and he made them a promise, but while Allah told the truth, he lied. He did not force them to follow him so Shaitan will tell them not to blame him but to blame themselves, he cannot help them, and they cannot help him. Not finding any help they will become angry with each other. The weak ones will ask those who they followed to help them against the punishment of Allah. But the ones they followed will say they were on the wrong path themselves, so how could they guide others?

The Angels guarding Hell will make fun of the people, reminding them they used to say Hell didn't even exist, and why don't they help each other now like they used to in the world? The people will beg for the Angels to pray for Allah to make their punishment less, even for one

day. But the Angels will ask them why they didn't follow the Prophets who were sent to them, who taught them how to save themselves from the punishment of Allah? The people will turn to the leader of the Angels of Hell, Malik, and beg him to ask Allah to let them die. He will reply that they will always remain in Hell. The people will cry, and when they run out of tears, blood will come out of their eyes.

Having no-one else to turn to, they will pray directly to Allah, for Allah to forgive them. Allah will make them wait a 1,000 years before He answers. Then He will tell them not to talk to Him, and the gates of Hell will be shut. When this happens, all hope will be lost, the worst punishment, and the people of Hell will begin braying like donkeys.

This is why the most important *Dua* we should make every day is for Allah to bless us to die as Muslims, because otherwise we will be of the losers, spending eternity in Hell.

O Allah, whomever among us You keep alive, then let such a life be upon Islam, and whomever among us You take unto Yourself, then let such a death be upon Iman (faith).[viii]
O Allah, protect us from the Hellfire.
O Allah, protect us from the Hellfire.
O Allah, protect us from the Hellfire[ix]

---

viii   Supplication from the funeral prayer for a deceased Muslim.

ix   The Prophet (peace be upon him) said: "Whoever asks Allah for Paradise three times, Paradise will say, 'O Allah, admit him to Paradise.' Whoever seeks protection from the Fire three times, Hell will say, 'O Allah, protect him from the Fire.'" (Tirmidhi)

Jannah

About *Jannah* (Paradise), Allah tells us that no person knows what is kept hidden for them as a reward for the good they used to do. The eight gates of Paradise will be opened, and the Angels will greet them. Upon entering Paradise, it has seven levels, each of which is unimaginably big and the distance between one level to another is like from the earth to the stars. Which level we end up in will be determined by our good deeds in this life and the mercy of Allah.

The garden given to each believer would take 100 years to explore. Within Paradise the trees are so huge that if a person was to ride their winged horses it would take 70 years to cross their shadow. There are rivers of milk, honey, wine[x] and water, and the trees are full of fruit, the types and tastes of which we have never seen or tasted. Birds of Paradise will eat from these fruits and these birds will also be food for the people.

The houses and tents will be made of gold, silver, pearls, diamonds, rubies, emeralds and sapphires. The sand is made of saffron, and clothes are made from silk. Each person will have their husband or wife from this world and from Paradise itself. They will be so beautiful that if their beauty was revealed to this world, it would fill it with light, and so sweet smelling that their scent would perfume the whole world.

The people of Paradise will always be comfortable, nothing will ever trouble them, and no-one will get unwell, grow old or die. They will be able to enjoy the company of their family, their ancestors and descendants, and the *Awliyah-Allah* and Prophets since the time of the Prophet Adam to our Prophet Muhammad (peace be upon them all).

Allah will speak to the people of Paradise, asking them if they are happy with everything He has given them. They will reply that of course they are happy. Allah will ask them if He should give them something even better than what He has already given them. The people will wonder and ask Allah, what can there be that is better than what they have already been given? Allah will tell them that

---

x   The wine of Paradise will not be like the wine of this world, but a refreshing drink which does not intoxicate or cause harm.

from now on He will always be happy with them. This blessing is so great that compared to it all the other special things of Paradise are like nothing – this is the purpose of our creation.

Even in Paradise Allah will be hidden, but from time-to-time Allah will look at the people of Paradise with love and let them see Him. This will be so amazing that when it happens the people will forget everything else and won't be able to look away. Then after a while Allah will again hide Himself and the people will go about their lives in Paradise. But they will not be able to forget how amazing it was to actually see Allah and will look forward to doing it again.

What can be more amazing than to be able to look upon Allah, for Him to be forever happy with us, to be able to spend time with the Prophets and *Awliyah-Allah*, and be with our friends and families in never-ending peace and comfort? This is why we should make a *Dua* every day for Allah to bless us to die as Muslims.

O Allah, whomever among us You keep alive, then let such a life be upon Islam, and whomever among us You take unto Yourself, then let such a death be upon Iman (faith).[xi]
O Allah, we ask You for Paradise.
O Allah, we ask You for Paradise.
O Allah, we ask You for Paradise.[xii]

---

xi   Supplication from the funeral prayer for a deceased Muslim.

xii The Prophet (peace be upon him) said: "Whoever asks Allah for Paradise three times, Paradise will say, 'O Allah, admit him to Paradise.' Whoever seeks protection from the Fire three times, Hell will say, 'O Allah, protect him from the Fire.'" (Tirmidhi)

Printed in Great Britain
by Amazon

19398042R00120